Overcoming Barriers To Church Growth

Steve Clapp

**ANDREW
CENTER
RESOURCES**

Overcoming Barriers To Church Growth

Steve Clapp

ISBN 0-9637206-3-5

Manufactured in the United States of America

This book is dedicated to the people who, through teaching, writing, and example, have taught me about church growth and about sharing the faith:

Walter Brueggemann	Kennon L. Callahan
Everett & Mary Jo Clapp	Howard Donahue
Carl S. Dudley	James W. Fowler
Ira Gallaway	Thomas H. Groome
Leroy Hodapp	Alvin Lindgren
John Robert McFarland	Loren B. Mead
Herb Miller	Paul Mundey
Jerry Peterson	Lyle Schaller
Norman Shawchuck	Richard Stolp
Walter Theobald	

And all the local churches who have sought my consulting help and in the process have become my teachers.

I also extend my appreciation for the valuable contributions made to the production of this book by Paul Mundey, Barb Faga, Karen Carlson, Carolyn Egolf, Holly Carcione, Jerry Peterson, and the staff of Evangel Press.

CONTENTS

"So if I, your Lord and Teacher, have washed your feet, you also ought to wash one another's feet. . . .

Very truly, I tell you, whoever receives one whom I send receives me; and whoever receives me receives him who sent me."

John 13:14, 20

A Familiar Story

"I don't understand all this talk about church growth. That's only one part of the life of the church. What about education? What about missions? What about the pastoral care of our existing members? In my opinion, if we do a good job with those things, then we won't have to worry about growth. We'll keep the people we already have, and we'll attract others by the quality of what we do."

Those words were spoken by a very astute, seventy-four-year old member of a church which had requested my consultive help in developing strategies for growth. What he shared, in fact, is a perspective not too different than that of several professors at the time I attended seminary in the late nineteen-sixties and early nineteen-seventies. While those of us in mainline denominations were aware that membership was declining, the rate of that decline had not yet alarmed us. What has become known by many as the "church growth movement" had gained momentum in some circles, but had not yet become such a major emphasis across virtually all denominations in the United States and Canada.

As we began examining data collected for the speaker's church and community, he was surprised to discover just how significant the membership decline had been and how much the age level composition of the church had changed. He readily agreed that what problems existed in the quality of the church programs were not sufficient to explain that level of loss in membership.

He was right to be concerned about the quality of pastoral care, education, missions work, and other programs in the life of the church. The standards of excellence maintained in his congregation were in fact impressive. Just maintaining quality programming, however, is not sufficient to maintain the existing level of membership or to reach out to those persons outside of the church.

His church had slid from well over four hundred members in 1973 to a little over two hundred members in 1993. The changes in age level distribution are vividly shown in the chart which follows:

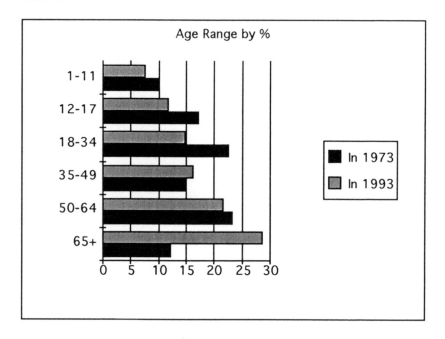

What has happened? Why isn't quality programming enough? The fact that you purchased or borrowed this book suggests that you already know some of the answers, which include factors like these:

1. While the percentage of people who believe in God has not changed significantly, the percentage who see active church involvement as an integral part of their faith has certainly declined. In a national study commissioned by *U.S. News and World Report* in March of 1994, eight out of every ten Americans surveyed shared a belief "that it's possible to be a good Christian

or Jew even without attending a church or synagogue" [*U.S. News*, p. 56]. Another recent study has shown that the majority of young adults [persons 18-35 years of age] feel that way - even if they personally are members of a church.

2. The increased mobility of society means that most people do not spend the rest of their lives in the same community in which they grew up. Loyalty to a local congregation which has been cultivated by quality programming doesn't help church membership when those persons move to other communities. Some people now experience so many relocations during their childhood that they are at a loss to identify a single "hometown."

3. Denominational loyalty has also substantially decreased over the past thirty years. People who are raised United Methodist do not necessarily remain United Methodist - or Evangelical Lutheran or Church of the Brethren or Disciples of Christ or just about any other denomination. When moving to a new community and choosing a new church home, people are increasingly likely to select a church based on the manner in which it meets their needs rather than because of the denomination with which it is affiliated.

4. Although it was once popular to speak about advances in technology creating more leisure time, the reality is that many people are incredibly busy. The days of a "typical family" including a husband who works and a wife who devotes her time to the household, the children, and civic causes are rapidly disappearing. We have increasing numbers of households with single parents or with both husband and wife working. Many jobs which pay well are very demanding and competitive, requiring large numbers of hours. A large proportion of the new jobs created, unfortunately, are part-time or temporary, with relatively low rates of pay and few benefits; thus some people find themselves working two or more jobs to make enough money. The demands of child care, home and yard maintenance, automobile care, grocery shopping, and other routine tasks leave many people feeling they don't have the time for church. Then, of course, there's the impact of television on people's time!

5. It was once widely assumed that people who left the church during the early part of their young adult years would return to involvement when they had children. While it remains true that becoming a parent often does make people think more

seriously about religious issues, return to church can no longer be assumed.

I could bombard you with statistics and devote many pages to expansion on the five reasons just shared as well as other factors which have made it a necessity for most of our churches to take seriously the need for church growth. Those factors, however, have been well articulated by other authors and are increasingly well-known. Journal articles, books, seminars, conferences, videos, and elaborate denominational programs have been reminding clergy, other church staff, and many lay leaders quite forcefully that church growth is important.

Yet huge numbers of local churches and most mainline denominations are in fact still showing significant rates of decline. The energy and commitment which have been applied to church growth initiatives, especially from the denominational level down, have in many instances not brought the desired results. Large numbers of churches are still trapped in cycles of aging and declining membership much like that of the church discussed at the beginning of this chapter, and many of those churches have members who love the church but truly do not know what to do about church growth.

In my book *Plain Talk About Church Growth* (first released in 1985 with a new edition in 1989), I offered a number of very practical strategies to help church leaders more effectively involve others in church growth. Response to that book continues to be very positive, and I've enjoyed talking with many pastors and other church leaders about their efforts to implement the strategies suggested by myself and by other consultants. As a result of those conversations and of my continued consultive work with many different congregations, I've developed a deeper appreciation for the barriers to growth which must be faced at the local church level. Failure to adequately address those barriers has limited the usefulness of many resources, including some of those which I've developed.

In this book, I've attempted to concisely and pragmatically address those barriers. The solutions which I offer will be effective in many situations and will hopefully stimulate your own thinking. As with every book on church administration and programming that I've written, I am very much indebted to the many local churches with which I've worked and to the many people who've taken the time to complete questionnaires and other research instruments for me.

Evangelism and Church Growth

Before beginning to address specific barriers to growth, I want to deal with the distinction which is often made between evangelism and church growth. Evangelism, as understood in most of our faith traditions, has to do with sharing the good news of Jesus Christ, and inviting others to know the joy and discipleship of the Christian faith. Properly understood, evangelism is carried out in the context of the larger mission of the church which includes acts of compassion and work for peace and justice.

Church growth centers on increasing the membership of local congregations and with generating accompanying gains in attendance, financial support, and leadership for many ministries of the church. Church growth certainly includes reaching those who are nonbelievers, but it also includes the development of strategies to reach persons who already see themselves as Christians but are not currently active in the life of a congregation.

On a personal level, I have not generally viewed evangelism and church growth as being in conflict with one another. While evangelism is traditionally more focused on the individual Christian than on the church as an institution, it is difficult for anyone to remain an effective, growing Christian in isolation from the church. I would be the first to argue that the body of Christ is not in every way identical with the church as an institution. Some of our local churches have compromised the faith, excluded others from Christian community, and treated people in ways completely inconsistent with the Gospel. For all the faults of the local church, however, it remains the most visible manifestation we have of the body of Christ.

Walter Bruggemann, in *Biblical Perspectives on Evangelism*, correctly reminds us that we have often missed the broader societal issues which are to be addressed in partnership with evangelistic activity. Caught up in efforts to see the faith shared with individuals and on efforts to increase the effectiveness of the local church, we sometimes fail to properly affirm our whole mission as the people of God. Bruggemann, who cares deeply about the church as an institution, reminds us that a biblical perspective on mission and evangelism really is not focused on the health of the institutional church. He argues that "the life of creation, the fabric of the human community, is deeply in jeopardy among us" [p.46]. While some people would argue that the threat of nuclear war is not quite as great today as in recent decades, that threat still exists. Beyond that, the ecological crisis, world hunger, violence, and human rights violations stand as significant dangers to all of us. The opening of The Holocaust Museum in Washington D.C. and the shocking reality of the motion picture *Schindler's List* are vivid reminders of just how thin the lines are which separate good from evil and humanity from inhumanity. The issues before us as Christians encompass not just the health of the church as an institution, but the health of the created world and of all humankind.

This book deals with church growth because that is the setting in which so many of us are deeply involved and the primary channel through which Christians share the faith and work for peace and justice. Our motivation, however, must run deeper than the desire to preserve the church as an institution.

And in all our work, we must remain ever aware that it is the power of God, not our own efforts, that transforms the hearts and minds of people and of nations. We are called to use the gifts we have received with intentionality, but God is not limited by our efforts and at times even chooses to work through our weaknesses rather than through our strengths.

The responsibility to be faithful witnesses for Christ and to work for the strengthening of the church as the body of Christ rests upon us, but we are not dependent on our own strength. The source of our power remains the risen Son.

Facing Reality:
Demographics and Growth

"I understand the importance of sharing the Gospel with others, and I suppose there are a few unchurched people in our little town. The reality for us, however, is that our population has been dropping steadily for thirty years; and I don't see anything that's going to bring many new people here. Even some of our retired farmers, who've been the backbone of this church, are starting to get tired of our horrible winters. The ones who can afford to move south are probably going to do it over the next four or five years. There's nothing to create new jobs here. The few people who have moved here in the last decade have mainly come for a job in the school system; and with the aging of the whole county, those openings are going to be few and far between the next several years."

"We sure need young adults in our church, but getting them seems an impossible task. Aside from the members who are college students and don't even live here except in the summer with their parents, we don't have any adults younger than forty and most of our members are over fifty. That puts us at a huge disadvantage in trying to gain younger members."

"We faced a difficult decision ten years ago. We knew that the neighborhood around the church was in transition and was going to become predominantly low income and black. We thought about moving the church east or north, where there's lots of new construction. After lots of debate, we decided to stay where we are. I'd like to say that we made the decision because we're committed to the neighborhood and want to become a multiracial congregation. That's part of the reason but not all of it. We couldn't agree on where to move the church, and we were

13

afraid of taking on the financial obligation of a new building. A lot of us kept hoping that the neighborhood wouldn't change as much as it has. . . Our pastor and his wife have been wonderful and have worked hard to help us become more open to the neighborhood. The reality, though, is that we haven't been able to bridge the cultural gap between our members who drive several miles to the church and the people who live within a few blocks of the church. There's not hostility, and people in the neighborhood participate in some of the seminars we offer, but we're just not what they're looking for in a church."

"This was my first experience starting a new congregation, and it's been the most meaningful of my career. At first I thought the denominational people were crazy when they put me here on salary but with no building and no staff and told me to spend nine months knocking on doors and recruiting a membership base. It was exhausting, but it worked! We held the first worship service in a school, and there were over two hundred people present. What a way to begin! There are lots of new housing starts around here, and most of the people are young families. Our biggest problem is how to assimilate new members because we're growing so fast."

"This is a gray-haired congregation, and we're proud of it. Most people move here to retire because the weather is so mild and the ocean's so close. The two bankers and three real estate agents who belong to our church keep directing new residents to us. Most of these people were active in local churches before they retired, and they want to stay involved. We have all kinds of programs for them, and we keep developing more all the time."

The first three persons quoted are in churches which are experiencing significant decline. The last two persons are in rapidly growing congregations. Characteristics of the population around those churches are having tremendous impact on their decline or growth. The existing characteristics of the churches themselves, in terms of ethnic background and dominant ages represented, impact the ease or the difficulty of reaching and assimilating new members.

Demography is the study of the characteristics of human populations such as size, rate of growth or decline, ethnic composition, and age level distribution. It's possible to take a demographic look at a local church, at a neighborhood or

14

ministry area served by a church, at cities, counties, states, and nations. The reality is that the demographic characteristics do play a major role in establishing the context in which ministry takes place. There are wonderful examples of local churches which are growing in spite of declining population around them, and there are sad examples of local churches which are declining even though the population around them is increasing. For most churches, however, the success of congregational outreach efforts is directly related to the demographics of the ministry area.

Loren B. Mead, in *More Than Numbers: The Way Churches Grow*, points out that "there are whole parts of the country in which church membership is likely to decline no matter what church leaders do" [p.40]. There are strategies which can be undertaken to work for growth in any situation, but there are also limitations which must be recognized.

For years, leaders in many denominations held up, as examples of effective evangelism and church growth, congregations which were located in areas experiencing rapid population growth. Local churches in other parts of the country were encouraged to utilize the same strategies which were successful in places of rapid population increase. Closer examination of those "model churches," however, often revealed that they had in fact not grown in membership as rapidly as the population in the surrounding area had increased. During the same period of time, some local churches located in communities with declining population were managing to maintain the same membership or were experiencing a rate of decline less than that in the community. The churches which were holding their own in spite of decline may have had more to teach than the model churches.

Virtually any consultant who visits a local church to conduct an evaluation and make recommendations for growth will ask people in the congregation to gather a significant amount of statistical information about the church and the community. Those figures are valuable in understanding the potential of the church and the best ways to reach out. Here are some key questions to consider as you seek to understand the potential in your particular situation:

1. Compare the present distribution of your congregation by

age level with that in your ministry area (the area from which most of the members of your congregation come). U.S. Census data is generally the best source of information about the community. What age levels, by percentage, are more strongly represented in your church than in the community? What age levels are underrepresented? A chart such as the following may be of help:

Age Level	# In Community	%	# In Church	%
0-11				
12-17				
18-34				
35-49				
50-64				
65+				

2. Consider the same data by marital status. This may help you identify categories of persons who are being missed by the church:

Status	# In Community	%	# In Church	%
Single				
Married				
Divorced				
Widowed				

3. If your ministry area has diversity in terms of ethnic background, compare the composition of the community with that of your church. To what extent has your congregation

attempted to reach out to persons of other ethnic backgrounds? To what extent do you think that is realistic in your situation?

4. Compare the rate of increase or decrease in the membership of your congregation over the last twenty years with the rate of increase or decrease of population in your ministry area. Are you holding your own? Are you gaining? Are you losing ground? Consider this in light of the answers to the first three questions. If you are gaining among particular groups or categories of people, what do you think are the reasons for those gains? If you are losing ground among particular groups or categories of people, what do you think are the reasons for those losses?

5. Identify the gains and losses in church membership over the past decade. How many people were gained through letter of transfer from other local congregations? Through letter of transfer from congregations in other communities (indicating these are people who moved to your community)? Through profession of faith? What are the ages of those gained?

How many were lost through death? Through letter of transfer to other congregations in the community? Through letter of transfer to congregations in other communities (indicating that these are people who moved away)? Through requesting that their names be removed from the church roster without transfer? What are the ages of those lost?

Comparing that information with the responses to the first four questions can help you gain a clearer image of what is happening in your church relative to the potential in your ministry area.

There are other resources, including many fine ones from denominational church growth and evangelism offices, which give more detailed help in gathering and evaluating demographic data. The purpose of the preceding questions is to help you begin thinking about demographic issues if you have not gathered such data in the past. Looking realistically at that data can lead you to several conclusions:

- That the potential for church growth in your ministry area is rather limited. You want to strategize ways to have the maximum possible impact, but you also must face the reality that only very superior programming and outreach will turn your membership

17

around. Future chapters will offer some help in that process, but it's good to begin with realistic expectations.

- That there are significant gaps between the groups of people represented in your church and those same groups of people (by age level, marital status, ethnic background) in your community. You should have the opportunity to develop positive strategies which will enable you to reach more of those persons. Again, future chapters will offer you specific help.

- That there are some potential barriers to growth because some groups in the community are so extremely underrepresented in the existing membership of your church. This can often be especially true with young adults, who are missing from so many congregations. Lacking a "core" of persons at a particular age level can make outreach more difficult - but there are strategies which can help. Keep reading!

Overcoming Low Self-Esteem

"I feel awkward asking someone to come to our church. We're so small that it doesn't seem like we have much to offer. There are only four or five kids in our youth group. We don't even have a choir for worship these days - just an occasional solo. I understand the need to reach out and get new people if our congregation isn't going to die, but it's hard to feel good about the process."

"Chris and Abby do a marvelous job inviting people to church. They're both such attractive people and so outgoing. I don't think people see me the same way, and I can't imagine someone accepting an invitation from a person like me. I want to help the church, but this friend-to-friend evangelism doesn't seem the right way for me."

"I used to dream about the day when I'd be pastoring one of the large churches in the denomination, but I know that isn't going to happen. My career has been okay, but I've not managed to accomplish anything great. I had three moves in a row that were basically parallel, and the move to this congregation was definitely a step down. At least I was honest with the search committee. They knew that I wouldn't be a fireball in the pulpit and that I probably wouldn't turn their church around. They have so many older members that they mainly were concerned about having someone who would be good to them and provide good pastoral care."

Both clergy and laity can suffer from low self-esteem about themselves or about their churches. That affects the willingness of people to reach out to others and also influences how proficiently the reaching out is done.

The first person quoted is painfully aware of the limitations of a small church: few people in the youth program, no choir, and limited opportunities for developing programs. That person has not learned how to recognize and share the benefits of being part of a small congregation - the fact that people do know and care about each other, the fact that new members can immediately become involved in leadership, and the fact that a small church offers many opportunities for people to make a difference in the lives of others and in the church. The reality is that the majority of local churches in the United States are small, and that enormous numbers of people find satisfaction in being part of a small congregation. Many people, including some youth, are uncomfortable being in large groups of people; and a small group may be very attractive. The church won't appear attractive, however, if those who are members see it in negative ways.

The second person quoted is no doubt not as outgoing as Chris and Abby. She understandably doesn't feel comfortable about friend-to-friend evangelism, and it is possible that her service to the church should come in other ways. Her statements, however, suggest that she sees herself as not especially attractive or interesting to others. The church certainly must recognize that some people are not going to be comfortable reaching out to nonmembers, but it's proper to be concerned about a person with such low self-esteem.

The third person quoted once had dreams of pastoring a large church but no longer sees himself as capable of that kind of accomplishment. Obviously people at the church to which he most recently moved feel that he has the ability to provide good pastoral care, or he would not have been invited to be their minister. He doesn't seem to attach as great significance to that as to his being less than a fireball in the pulpit. Low self-esteem from the pastor of a church often infects the members of the church as well.

For the most part, prospective members are not drawn to churches or individuals with low self-esteem. People want to feel good about themselves, and they are more likely to seek relationships with churches and individuals who have healthy self-esteem.

When asked what people must do to have eternal life, our Lord responded:

> **You shall love the Lord your God with all your heart, and with all your soul, and with all your strength, and with all your mind; and your neighbor as yourself.**
> **[Luke 10:27]**

If love of one's self is the standard by which one is encouraged to love others, then low self-esteem sets limitations on how loving we can be toward other people. Those who feel good about themselves are better equipped to help *others* feel good about themselves.

Obviously arrogance and the wrong kind of pride are inconsistent with the Christian faith, but low self-esteem can also be a problem because it separates us from the best in ourselves and keeps us at times from seeking the best in others. The opposite of pride may seem to be humility, but it in fact is often shame.

Low self-esteem not only relates to individual lives and to the local church, but also to feelings about and within denominations. Consider these statements from people in different denominations:

"Sometimes I wonder what hope there is for a denomination like ours. Nobody has heard of us. We're not like the Methodists or the Lutherans or the Catholics that everyone knows about. The fact that so few people outside the denomination have even heard of us is a big barrier in church growth."

"I used to be proud of being a Methodist, I mean *United* Methodist, but I don't feel that way now. We're such a big, inclusive denomination that there's nothing distinctive about us. I feel like people are looking for churches that have clear beliefs and that draw firm lines between what's right and what's wrong. I don't know how to explain who we are to someone outside the church."

"Trying to explain my denomination to others can be an exercise in frustration and rejection. There's an official church position on everything, and some of those positions are a turnoff, especially for young adults. I don't know why faith in Christ can't be enough. Why do we have to be so rigid that we exclude people?"

Some smaller denominations are especially likely to have low self-esteem precisely because they are not widely known in the United States or Canada. As the second quote about denominational identity indicates, however, large denominations are not immune to that problem. It's also interesting to note that the United Methodist feels beliefs within his denomination aren't sufficiently clear, while the last person quoted feels that the rigid beliefs of her denomination keep people away.

My conversations with clergy and laity in churches which are growing and with those in churches which are not growing leave me increasingly convinced that low self-esteem is a far greater barrier to church growth than has generally been recognized. It also keeps those who are already church members from achieving the satisfaction which should come to them through their church membership.

Low Personal Esteem

My guest and I sat down at a church dinner across from two people who had been present for at least fifteen minutes before our arrival. I knew one of the people who was a member of the church but did not know the other. I introduced myself and my guest to the person I did not know and then introduced my guest to the church member. Then I realized that these two people had been sitting side-by-side, but had not exchanged introductions or conversation. Following my initiative, they began talking together and discovered that they had a great deal in common.

From my perspective, the person who belonged to the church had the primary obligation to reach out to the visitor but failed to do so. What does that mean? That the church member was cold or aloof? While that would certainly appear to be one interpretation, it is an incorrect one. I know that person to be a warm person who genuinely cares about others. That the church member was shy? That's a possibility in this instance, and it's important to remember that shyness is not always the same as low self-esteem. Shyness can be the result of a reserved or cautious nature in reaching out to others, and that isn't identical with having a low opinion of one's self. In that particular situation, however, the shyness of the church member was a reflection of low self-esteem.

People who don't feel good about themselves are often reluctant to reach out to others. While that church member does generally feel warmly toward others and has shown significant concern for others, she nevertheless struggles with a very low self-image and has fairly frequent problems with depression. If her self-esteem were greater, she would no doubt reach out more comfortably to others and would also project greater genuine warmth and concern.

It's important to emphasize again that shyness and low self-esteem do not always go together. Some people simply are more introverted than others, and that is not a negative characteristic. People who may be shy about initial introductions and conversations may often be people who have the ability to cultivate relationships to genuine depth and sharing.

Low self-esteem, however, is a very common problem and does affect how people tend to feel about the way they'll be perceived by others and how they feel about the organizations to which they belong. Whole courses have been developed by many organizations to help people increase their self-esteem. The following checklist may be helpful to you in thinking about the extent to which you or others are plagued by low self-esteem:

Do you (or the person about whom you are concerned):

_____ feel reluctant to meet new people because you have a strong fear that they will not feel positively about you?

_____ spend a great deal of time criticizing yourself for mistakes?

_____ find it difficult to accept the sincerity of compliments which you receive?

_____ feel reluctant to phone people you've known for years to ask them for a favor because you fear that you are imposing, even though you've often done similar things for them?

_____ find yourself readily accepting the blame almost every time that you have a problem in a relationship with someone?

_____ feel reluctant to complain when you've received what feels like poor service in a restaurant or a retail store because you fear that you may have done something to deserve it?

_____ find it almost impossible to list ten things which you genuinely like about yourself?

_____ fairly consistently feel that the value of your work for the church is not as great as the value of the work done by most other people?

_____ assume when you have trouble understanding a speaker, a television program, or a book that the reason is probably because you aren't intelligent enough to grasp what is being communicated?

_____ have a tendency to develop addictions to substances like alcohol, tobacco, or illegal drugs?

_____ have many times when you feel angry with yourself for the inability to change behaviors or patterns of thinking which really upset you?

_____ have trouble accepting the reality that God loves you, has truly forgiven your sins, and does not expect you to in some way "earn" your salvation?

_____ find yourself being very sloppy about matters of personal appearance, feeling as though it doesn't really make any difference?

_____ feel reluctant to volunteer for many things in the church out of fear that you won't do the work well enough?

_____ find it perfectly normal that an organization
to which you belong fails to maintain high
standards of quality?

_____ often feel tempted to lie or to slightly distort
the truth in order to make yourself appear
more interesting or exciting to other people?

None of the preceding characteristics alone means that you
or another person has low self-esteem. If you found yourself
checking more than a few of the items, however, it is quite
possible that self-esteem is a problem.

How do you overcome low self-esteem and help others do the
same? There are many potential strategies, and there are some
seminars and workshops which give help in enhancing self-
esteem. Here are some ideas and perspectives worth considering:

• Find a person you trust and whom you believe has
  a positive image of you (or at least as positive an
  image as you feel it likely anyone will have). Tell
  this person that you are working to improve your
  self-image and that you would like to get together
  once every week or two to monitor your progress.
  Then begin sharing with this person your struggles
  to feel better about yourself. In some instances,
  this kind of strategy may be as useful to you as
  psychological counseling, though it is not likely
  to work if there are deeper problems underlying
  your low self-esteem.

• Buy a spiral notebook and start a journal. On
  the first day's entry, write down ten things that
  you like about yourself. This may seem difficult
  at first, but keep working at it. Then write in your
  journal on a daily basis if possible or at least
  three times a week. Make yourself record one
  positive thing which you've accomplished each
  time you write in the journal.

• Read helpful books like David Reynolds' *Playing
  Ball on Running Water*; Scott Peck's *Further Along
  the Road Less Traveled*; or Chris Schriner's *Feel
  Better Now*. Classes or groups can be established

in the church for the discussion of these or
similar resources.

• If addiction is a problem, join one of the twelve-
step support groups in your community and seek
the help of that organization in overcoming the
dependency.

• Pray to God for help in better understanding your
spiritual gifts and abilities. Do this on a daily
basis with a genuine effort to open yourself to
God's guidance and love.

• Utilize one of the spiritual gifts inventory programs
available through your own church or through
another source. Those by the Church Growth
Institute, Herb Miller's Net Results organization,
and Bruce Bugbee's Networking Resources are
all excellent. Understanding your spiritual
gifts almost always results in enhanced self-
esteem.

• Learn something new! Pick one thing that you've
always wanted to do and start learning how to do
it! Few things increase self-worth like learning
how to do something you couldn't accomplish
in the past.

• Make yourself 3" X 5" notecards with sayings
like the following on them, and put them in your
pocket, billfold, or purse, so that you can review
them several times each day:

> **God made me, and God doesn't make
> mistakes!**

> **I can do all things through Christ who
> strengthens me.**

> **I am a child of God for whom Christ died
> on the cross, and that makes me of
> enormous worth.**

Each person I encounter today will be just as concerned about having my approval as I will be about having his or her approval.

While there is much wrong with being prideful in the sense of being arrogant toward others or feeling superior to others, there is nothing wrong and a great deal right about having healthy pride in the things one has accomplished.

- Develop a program to improve your physical appearance over the next three months. Have someone take a photograph of you at the start of the program, and then take another photograph at the end. Feeling better about physical appearance generally brings an overall improvement in self-esteem.

- If none of the strategies described here seem workable to you, or if you try some of them without success, then you may wish to seek the counsel of a minister, a psychologist, a psychiatrist, or a social worker who specializes in self-esteem issues.

The local church can help members of the congregation with self-esteem issues in a number of ways including:

- The provision of checklists and suggestions similar to those just shared.

- The formation of study groups to deal with self-esteem questions.

- The use of sermons to help people distinguish between the kind of pride which is inconsistent with the Christian faith and the healthy self-esteem which all people need.

- The formation of programs and classes to help people identify their spiritual gifts and then apply those in the ministry of the church.

Low Congregational Esteem

"It's nice that you're willing to stay this late and visit, but I for one don't see anything that can be done to help us. I think it's a shame that the denomination sent us a pastor as enthusiastic as Mike. Someone that young and full of energy is wasted on a church like ours. If he stays here two or three years, it'll be a wonder if he has any enthusiasm left. I don't know why anyone would want to be pastor of this congregation. The people are nice enough, but you can't get them to do anything. They want to come to worship services, put a few dollars in the offering plate, and get out of church in time to beat the brunch crowd at the restaurants in town."

The speaker was a middle-aged woman who had grown up in that congregation. I was working in church bureaucracy at the time and had just finished conducting an informational meeting on a major pensions and camping fund drive. The meeting had been held in her church and was attended by representatives from about fifty other congregations. At the conclusion of the program, their new pastor had asked me to visit informally with six leaders in the church about the continuing decline of their membership and their problems raising the needed funds to support their budget.

"I don't think it's quite that hopeless," said a man in his sixties who was the president of a small bank near the church and who had also grown up in that congregation. "We had all agreed that we needed a younger pastor; and, in my opinion, we were lucky to get Mike. This 'friend-to-friend' program he's starting to push seems like a good way to draw people into the church. I know a lot of people in town, but I just haven't thought before about inviting them to church."

"But we tried something almost exactly like that ten or fifteen years ago, Bill," responded a woman who was also in her sixties. "You meet a lot of people at the bank, but most of us don't know that many folks. Besides that, when you start asking, you'll find that almost everyone already belongs to a church. And you can't get most of our people to take that big an interest."

"I can think of people to invite," said the husband of the middle-aged woman. "The problem I see is that getting them here once or twice isn't enough. We have to get them interested enough to keep coming and to join the church. They'll respond well enough to Mike. He's a good preacher, and he makes people feel welcome. But look at our Sunday school and our youth program. Those aren't going to keep anybody coming who has children."

"Bob and Karen are starting to turn the youth program around," their pastor offered. "They had seven kids at the hot dog roast last weekend. That's not a big crowd, but it's a big improvement over the three or four we were having - and over all the weeks when no one came."

"But look at our financial problems," said a woman in her late twenties, the youngest person in the group. She turned toward me as she made the rest of her comments. "We're getting enough in donations to pay Mike and the utility bills, but we're not current on anything else. We're behind on the payments we're supposed to make to the denomination, and you come tonight saying that we need to raise money for pensions and camping. I've got news for you! We're lucky to get enough money to keep the doors of this church open. Building up the youth program and getting new people to come may help us in the long run, but we've got to keep the church going right now. I had no idea how bad it was until I became treasurer."

All congregations have some members whose personal self-esteem is low. The church just described by its key leadership is dealing with a slightly different reality, which is that the church itself, as a body of people, is experiencing low self-esteem. The two kinds of low self-esteem, of course, may be closely related. If many members of a church suffer from personal low self-esteem, then it's not surprising that the congregation as a whole develops a negative self-image or low self-esteem.

Of course there are churches in situations of declining population and a poor economic environment which deal with problems of such a magnitude that it may be difficult to avoid a certain measure of low self-esteem. The church just described, however, was not in that kind of situation. The population base in the ministry area served by that church had remained relatively stable for twenty years; and while the community was

29

not overly prosperous, income levels were reasonable and unemployment was not high. That is the case in the majority of situations where churches are suffering from low self-esteem. In such churches, the low self-esteem itself becomes a major problem blocking growth and improved health. It's likely that low congregational self-esteem is one of the barriers to growth for your church if several of the following are true:

- Key leaders complain that the majority of members are apathetic and do not care about the church.

- The budget of the church for the past five years has barely managed to increase enough to keep pace with inflation, even though the local economic situation is not significantly worse than for the country as a whole.

- Many of the current members of the church are inactive, and no one can readily identify any key events or reasons which are responsible for the inactivity.

- A large number of members are quick to respond to most suggestions for innovation or improvement by saying things like: "That won't work here." "People won't support that." "You can't get people here to do that."

- People frequently respond to a suggestion for improvement by referring to a similar attempt which was made many years ago and did not work.

- People continue to talk positively about a pastor of fifteen or more years ago as though that individual were the standard for measuring everything today.

- People are very reluctant to accept leadership positions because they feel it will be next to impossible to get others to help.

- Most of the effort and money of the church goes to institutional maintenance rather than to any kind of outreach or mission.

- There is a major dependency on the pastor and any other paid staff for both initiation and implementation of programs.

- There is a reasonably deep conviction among leadership that getting the right pastor will turn the church around, and the initial enthusiasm over a new pastor quickly disappears when it becomes clear that person will not be performing any miracles.

- Problems with finances are a frequent topic of discussion, and the solution to most financial problems is to cut back on spending rather than to find a way to generate more income.

- One or two very dominating leaders are permitted to exercise an excessive amount of control over decisions which are made.

- When people are heard talking about their church to those outside the congregation, the comments are likely to be of a negative, disappointed, or powerless nature.

- Relatively little is done to celebrate the positive things that happen in the life of the church such as a Vacation Bible School program, the successful completion of the church school year, the work of the choir, the efforts of Sunday school teachers, the elimination of a debt, the renovation of the parsonage, or the birth of a child.

- The church's physical facilities have been permitted to deteriorate and have an overall feel of neglect. (This can be a very serious sign, because most churches will expend at least some money on physical facilities even if they won't give the pastor a raise or support missions! The building reflects directly on the people of the congregation.)

When a church has low congregational self-esteem, it becomes very difficult to reach out to new members. If people don't feel enthusiastic about the church themselves, how are they going to successfully interest other people? When the only motivations for going after new members are to gain more money and volunteer time for the church, it's almost impossible to create the kind of caring atmosphere and genuine concern for others which people hope to find in a church home. There are, fortunately, several strategies which can be utilized to help improve the self-esteem of a congregation.

1. The pastor and other key leaders must become aware that the congregation is suffering from low self-esteem. Without an awareness that low congregational self-esteem is presenting a barrier to church growth, it's easy for leaders to attempt the implementation of strategies which will actually further decrease the church's self-esteem. Too much emphasis on the problems of the church will further depress people and make them even less enthusiastic than previously to reach out to others.

2. The pastor, key lay leadership, and (sometimes) a consultant from outside the congregation need to help in the process of a realistic assessment of the church - with an emphasis on strengths. The problems in the church certainly need to be identified - but the same process which identifies the weaknesses also needs to identify the strengths of the congregation. An outside consultant is not always necessary for that task, but such a person can often speed up the process, and the enthusiasm of that individual may help the church's enthusiasm. The consultant could be a person who specializes in such work for his or her living, a caring member of denominational staff, or a neighboring pastor.

The more people from the congregation who can be involved in the assessment process, the better. While weaknesses and problems usually do need to be identified, it is crucial to emphasize the strengths of the church. In his classic book *Twelve Keys to an Effective Church*, Kennon Callahan writes: "Realistically knowing and strongly affirming those strengths that the church 'has going for it' is decisive for success. Substantial power is generated as a congregation discovers and claims its strengths" [p. xvi].

After I had listened to over thirty minutes of the six church leaders telling me everything that was wrong with their congregation, I pushed them to start identifying all the things that were good about their church and about their ministry area. At first it took considerable pushing on my part and that of their pastor, but then they warmed to the task. Their list included:

- A young, enthusiastic minister.

- Mike's enthusiasm was generating positive comments in the community.

- Four young adults, including the new treasurer, who were beginning to assume more leadership.

- An improved youth program.

- A lot of teenagers in the community, without any apparent church home, who could be prospective members.

- A large building, in reasonably good repair, with plenty of available space for programs.

- A reasonably stable community population.

- The membership decline had been steady but not really rapid.

- No rich members but several people capable of giving more to the church.

- Two fairly large adult Sunday school classes.

- Three members, including the banker, who were in positions to meet newcomers to the community.

- When a death occurred in a church family, there was a tradition of providing a meal for the family and others attending the funeral.

- Choir members had new, attractive robes (funded by a barbecue the past summer).

- Young people who were not members of the church nevertheless liked to have wedding services performed

33

there.

- While many members were apathetic about church growth, they were not unfriendly or cold to people who visited the church.

- Several retired members who were good cooks and who would probably be willing to bake cookies or bread which could be taken to those who visited worship services.

- A growing awareness on the part of members that growth is important.

- A Sunday school that was fully staffed each year (even though that required a lot of effort!).

3. Though the pastor can't be expected to turn the church around alone, a proactive stance and a positive style by the pastor can have significant impact. Mike, in fact, played a major role in turning around the church just described. At the time I visited with the six people involved in leadership, some initially expressed disappointment that having a pastor as enthusiastic as Mike had not brought about quicker changes in the life of the church. As they began to realistically look at what had happened, however, they began to recognize that they were expecting change more rapidly than was realistic and that their own disappointment was not helpful to Mike or the church.

There is a general tendency in churches to overestimate the amount of change which can be accomplished in a single year and to underestimate the amount of change which can take place in five years. The minister plays a major role in setting the climate for change and innovation in the church. While it's important for the pastor to be realistic about the limitations and weaknesses of the church and the community, staff leadership can play an extremely valuable role in helping members develop a greater appreciation for one another and for the potential of the church. If the minister does not give up too quickly and encourages other people to keep building on the strengths of the church, growth can happen.

The minister and other staff can also perform valuable roles as cheerleaders. The accomplishments of the church need to be celebrated, and those who work in the church need to be rewarded for their efforts. There should be celebration of improvements to facilities, of youth mission trips, of Vacation Bible School completion, and of other church accomplishments. There should also be celebration of births, weddings, anniversaries, and the addition of new members. The work of choir members, ushers, and church school teachers should be recognized in a way that reminds all members of the church that good things are happening.

4. The initiation of a spiritual gifts program can bring improved self-esteem and enthusiasm to individuals and to the church as a whole. Spiritual gift identification was discussed some under suggestions for improving individual self-esteem. The good programs in this area help people more clearly identify the gifts they have been given and the ways that those may be used in the life of the church. This can be a very energizing process for a congregation.

5. The church needs to set specific, attainable, measurable goals and work for their completion. Success nurtures more success. Rather than taking on *all* the weaknesses identified for a congregation, identify specific, positive changes which can be made - either correcting existing weaknesses or building on strengths. The church described earlier in this section ended up identifying and accomplishing the following:

- Training a minimum of fifteen people in how to do friend-to-friend evangelism. (Twenty-three people were actually trained.)

- Putting a new, larger sign at the front of the church with room for the sermon title to be displayed or for specific events to be promoted.

- Developing a church brochure which highlighted what the congregation had to offer new members.

- Changing the church's advertisement in the yellow pages to one which included information on child care.

- Painting and making other improvements to the Sunday school classrooms, the restrooms, and the nursery to reflect greater pride in the church.

- Having a special fund-raising dinner to pay for the employment of a college intern during the summer to help the church conduct a special outreach to teenagers.

- Having "cottage meetings" in homes in connection with the church's stewardship drive to talk about the good things happening in the church and to solicit suggestions from members for further improvements.

- Including in each issue of the monthly newsletter a box with a suggestion about inviting others to church.

- Taking two Sundays a year on which members are urged during the worship service to write on a notecard the names of three people they know who are not members of a local church. They are urged to pray for those persons and are given suggestions for reaching out to them personally with information about the church.

- Developing a program through which visitors to worship services or Sunday school receive a visit within forty-eight hours, including the gift of homemade cookies or bread.

- Stopping the practice of having "panic talks" about church finances during worship. This helped the worship service itself be more positive and also avoided causing visitors to feel that the church was after their money.

6. Improve the quality of care and nurture for existing members both by the pastors and by others. High quality pastoral care helps people feel good about the church and also helps them feel good about themselves. In most congregations, this means that both employed staff and volunteers need to be involved in outreach to persons in hospitals and nursing homes, as well as to those who are confined in their own homes or who are dealing with other problems.

Sloppy pastoral care makes people think they are not important to the church and also lowers their opinion of the church as an organization. If people are going to be enthusiastic about the church, it's important for them to feel well cared for by the church.

Denominational Self-Esteem

"It's hard for me to be a good Catholic these days. I don't even know what it means. The priest we have now is not nearly as progressive as the last one. Which one of them is right? What am I supposed to believe?"

"I get distressed because some people have never even heard of the Church of the Brethren. The people I talk with often say 'Oh, didn't you have a merger with the Methodists?' What they're thinking about is the Evangelical United Brethren, who did have a merger with the former Methodist Church to form the United Methodist Church. We're such a small denomination by comparison to the Methodists or the Baptists or the Disciples. What's the point of talking to people who haven't heard of us?"

"I sometimes think that calling ourselves a Presbyterian church is a mistake. People around here seem to have these set ideas of what a Presbyterian is. They think we're mainly upper class and that we're liberals on social issues. That's really not who we are at all, but it's hard to explain that. Maybe we should just call ourselves First Community Church."

The preceding statements reflect frustration about various aspects of the denominations of the speakers. Those frustrations don't always translate into low denominational self-esteem; but as with the same statements near the beginning of this chapter, the potential for that exists.

We are in the midst of a difficult period of time for most of the mainline denominations. Memberships have been declining, and members have grown increasingly critical of denominational offices and policies. This in turn has caused a defensive reaction from many denominational executives. The overall question of how denominations should respond to these changing, high pressure times would require a separate book. Here are some brief suggestions which have potential for helping at the denominational and the local church level. These are certainly not original and have been positively implemented in many places.

1. At the denominational level, there should be a continuing emphasis on providing attractive interpretive resources for use by local congregations. These may include print materials, videocassettes, and positive commercials and programs for radio and television use. These can appropriately highlight strengths of the denomination, examples of important ministries, or community service information. Some materials certainly need to address such basic questions as:

- What does it mean to be a Roman Catholic today?

- What is the Church of the Brethren?

- What are the major beliefs of the United Methodist Church?

Major beliefs and positions of denominations need to be presented in positive ways. Some denominations have clear statements of their beliefs and positions on a wide range of theological and social issues. Other denominations may take a more open stance and even actively encourage diversity. Those which take a more open stance need to say more about the encouragement of diversity - making the openness an asset rather than a liability.

2. Denominational executives need to be careful not to interpret all requests for change as criticisms. As already discussed, there is an understandable tendency for executives in denominational offices to become defensive when being criticized by pastors and local church leaders. Yet those who remain in the denomination and work for change should be seen as friends rather than enemies. People who have given up on the denomination don't stay around to work for change.

While requests for change or explanation and outright criticisms are sometimes unfair or based on incorrect information, a nondefensive posture toward those raising the questions is the best way to build confidence and to promote a more positive image. The link between denominational offices, programs, and missions and the local congregation is of critical importance and needs to be nurtured everywhere possible. Anything which denominational staff can do to provide high quality service to local congregations will go a long way in improving denominational loyalty. In many instances, denominations need to be providing more direct services to local churches rather than developing large programs and asking churches to "buy into" them.

Some congregations do change their names to avoid immediate connection to the parent denomination on the part of prospective members. While many people are uncomfortable with that trend, the reality is that several congregations do feel more comfortable being known as St. Matthew's Church, First Community Church, Mt. Zion Church, or Lakewoods Church than having a denominational adjective inserted. As long as there is a healthy link between the denomination and the church, however, that should not be viewed as a problem. People sometimes do have preconceptions about what a particular denomination is like, and those preconceptions can be barriers. Churches which take that stance with their name, however, need to be sure that interpretive information which does indicate the denominational affiliation gets shared with prospective members fairly early in the process, so that those persons do not feel they have been misled.

3. Persons in small denominations should not be overly concerned with the issue of name recognition. Certainly from the perspective of a small denomination, it may seem that larger denominations have an immediate advantage with the better name recognition which they enjoy. As some of the quotes shared in this chapter show, however, the immediate name recognition may also carry along an assortment of assumptions about the denomination which may not be true at all for a specific local church. The fact that a denomination is not well-known provides an opening for conversation with prospective members and may in fact result in clearer communication.

4. Both the denominational and the local church levels need to identify the most distinctive features they have and highlight those in interpretive materials. No church can be all things to all people. Being clear about the uniqueness of a denomination and a local church makes it easier for persons without church homes to make informed choices and also keeps those involved in the recruitment of members from wasting time on persons who will not be happy if they do join the church.

The local churches and denominations with which I am personally most familiar are all conducting or supporting important ministries of many different kinds. Those need to be highlighted and can greatly enhance the image of the church and the denomination.

5. Local churches need to interpret the nature of the denomination to existing members. This can be done through printed materials, sermons, classes, and special seminars. Church members are often uncomfortable about denominational affiliations simply because they do not understand the distinctive teachings of the denomination. Providing that information frees people to be better advocates of the church.

Overcoming
Negative Attitudes

Negative attitudes obviously can be a major barrier to church growth. Those attitudes are often a reflection of low self-esteem on the part of the individual or of the church. Whenever possible, deal with those attitudes in a systemic way by working to improve self-esteem in individuals and the church.

There will, of course, be times when negative attitudes emerge and must be responded to immediately. Here are some common statements which flow out of negative attitudes along with strategies for dealing with them:

That won't work here. Explain with care the positive reasons for which you believe that it will work. Be as specific as possible. Then talk about the "worst case scenario" - what is the worst thing that will happen if you try what has been suggested? When talking about the church growth area, generally speaking, the most likely negative consequence of a strategy failing is simply that you do not get the new members you wanted. If the church is already not getting as many new members as are wanted and needed, there's no serious negative consequence to trying something that doesn't work.

Another approach to the "that won't work here" complaint is to try something on a trial basis. Experiment with a Friday or Saturday evening worship service for six months, and then evaluate the result. Involve six people in a "friend-to-friend" evangelism emphasis. If the process is successful, then open the training to the whole church. Run newspaper advertisements for three months, and then evaluate the results.

While it is sometimes best to avoid direct confrontation and to give those who state opposition to a new idea the opportunity to graciously go along with an experimental period of time, you may need to push those persons for specifics about why they feel something won't work. Perhaps they do see problems which you haven't anticipated. Perhaps the barriers only exist in their minds.

Be sure people really do have the full picture of why something is needed. The Education Commission in one church proposed a very ambitious fall program, designed to reach more children and utilizing a part-time staff person. Board members expressed some hesitation on the basis that the educational effort would take the time and energy of so many additional volunteers in addition to requiring fund raising for the part-time staff member. The Commission shared the chart which follows to remind people of how much change there had been in Sunday school enrollment at the children's level:

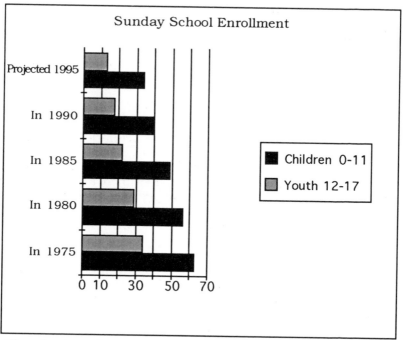

The chart made it clear that something had to be done. The alternative would be to see enrollments continue to decline. Until seeing the chart, many people had simply failed to be aware of the seriousness of the situation.

We tried that before. This kind of negative thinking assumes that because something didn't work once, it shouldn't be tried again. Much of the time, however, what was previously attempted will turn out to have been different than the current proposal. The first strategy in dealing with this barrier is to ask for specifics about what was attempted in the past and why that effort failed. Ask for details and carefully record them on a chalkboard or newsprint. The process of requesting the specifics shows that you are taking the person seriously and trying to understand, which often lowers hostility. Then go through and identify the ways in which your current proposal and current situation are different than in the past. You may even identify some changes which can be made in the proposal which will make it more likely to be accepted.

Several people in a congregation were opposed to doing neighborhood canvassing with information about the church because of a past house-to-house effort during which some people had received hostile comments from persons in the neighborhood. On the basis of those concerns, the church decided to make the new effort a more successful one by: (1) having people work in teams of two for mutual reinforcement and support; (2) providing more careful training than had been done in the past; and (3) having the opening questions ones which immediately determined whether or not someone was already active in a church and leaving them with good wishes for their continued activity. Specific discussion showed that the problems in the past had primarily been related to people not knowing how to start conversations and in a few instances not finding out someone already had a church home until embarrassingly late in the conversation.

There's no money in the budget for this, and it's going to be too expensive. This is a powerful phrase because it can destroy an idea without any serious consideration of the merits of the strategy. "There's not enough money" will sink many ideas and turn off the creativity of those involved. The objection can be a serious one, but there are several possible strategies. (1) Be sure that cost estimates are as realistic and as low as possible. If you're dealing with purchase of advertising time on the radio, for example, find out if the cost can be lowered by making a longer commitment at the time. It may also be possible to proceed on a smaller scale to find out if a strategy will be effective. (2) Ask for permission to do a special offering or a special fund-raising effort to raise the needed money. (3) Postpone the idea until the next budget year if there is no way to finance it properly in the current year.

That will be too big a change for this church. It's difficult to differentiate between this kind of concern coming as a result of negative thinking and coming as a result of realistic thinking. You need to think about and talk with others about these questions: (1) How many other changes are in process in the church right now? Does that make this a good time or a bad time for another change? (2) How thoroughly have the people who will be affected been involved in talking about the potential change? If they have not been involved, then it's difficult to know how valid the criticism is that the change will be too big. Seek input from those persons, and also interpret to them why the change is needed. (3) Consider, again, the possibility of making the change on a trial or experimental basis to give everyone involved opportunity to see how successful it is. (4) Be sure to clearly present what the results will be of failure to change. If a church is rapidly losing members, then there may be no realistic alternative.

The _____ group will never go along with that. This objection often comes as a result of someone feeling he or she knows how another group in the church is likely to respond. The best approach, almost always, is to go directly to that group, explain the desired change carefully, and then attempt to gain their support. If the proposed innovation is important, don't simply accept one person speaking for a whole group which hasn't discussed an idea.

The district executive or bishop or moderator or. . . will never approve of that. The appeal to higher authority can be a powerful weapon in stopping innovation, if those present have the perception that the speaker has a good understanding of how the higher authority is likely to respond. One of the first questions to ask is whether or not the higher authority actually should be consulted about the matter. If it is appropriate to consult with the higher authority or if that is actually a requirement for implementation, then the best response to this objection is generally to suggest that the higher authority be permitted to make the determination. Those who offer appeal to that authority more as threat than as logical argument will often withdraw their objection.

Overcoming a Shortage Of Volunteers

Having an insufficient number of volunteers can be a significant barrier to church growth. Virtually any church growth effort that is not totally staff-dependent needs volunteers to help reach out to potential members and to respond to those who start visiting worship and other congregational activities. Churches also need volunteers to maintain the kinds of quality programs which will be attractive to potential members and which will nurture present membership. The following ideas and perspectives may be helpful to you in this process:

- Consider the implementation of a spiritual gifts program, as described in the chapter on self-esteem. That kind of program can put people in touch with their gifts and change their work in the church from obligation into opportunity. The full implementation of such a program is a long-term strategy, but can be effective for every phase of the life of the church.

- Be sure that existing church leadership is fully aware of the need for church growth. If your church has been in decline for many years, provide statistics, possibly in chart form, which show what has been happening. Also focus attention on growth or decline in membership at various age levels. The kinds of information discussed in the chapter on demographics can be helpful in this regard. Having church leaders aware of these concerns can help motivate more of them to put energy into church growth concerns.

- Talk with your church's nominating committee or volunteer recruitment committee about the importance of growth for the future of your church. Urge them to make church growth a priority in their recruitment efforts.

- Offer people a variety of ways in which they can help with church growth efforts. Some people will be more attracted to certain tasks than to others. Think about the different people who might be willing to:

  - Circulate on Sunday morning during a coffee/ fellowship time to be sure that visitors are introduced to members.

  - Bake cookies or bread which can be taken to first-time visitors.

  - Deliver cookies or bread to first-time visitors.

  - Canvass neighborhoods with information about your church.

  - Write articles for the church newsletter.

  - Maintain accurate records about visitors to worship, Sunday school, and other church functions.

  - Be a "faith friend" to a prospective member, nurturing that person through from the status of a second or third time visitor to a member of the congregation.

  - Serve on a coordinating committee that deals with overall issues of church growth.

  - Make phone calls to encourage people to come to church.

  - Develop a brochure or other print materials about your church.

  - Help make radio or television advertising arrangements.

- If your church organization or program includes prayer groups or prayer chains, ask those persons to pray for growth for your congregation and for sufficient volunteers to be identified. Prayer works,

and having a large number of persons aware of the
need for volunteers also helps.

- Be sure that you provide positive feedback and
  encouragement to those who do volunteer work
  (for church growth or for anything else in the
  congregation). People need to know that their work
  is appreciated and that they are making a difference
  for the church.

- Have those persons who are already active in church
  growth or evangelism efforts identify other persons who
  might be positively involved. If the persons already
  working in these areas feel enthusiastic about a
  potential volunteer, that makes it more likely that
  he or she will agree to help.

- Don't overlook tasks which can be done by committed
  teenagers. In addition to reaching out to other students,
  they can also do canvassing and deliver baked goods.

- Newer members of your congregation are often the
  people who will be most enthused about reaching out
  to prospective members. There is a natural tendency
  to overlook those persons because they are new, and
  that is generally a mistake. They need to be involved
  in the ministries of the church, and they may be
  especially excellent ambassadors for the church.

- Try to avoid recruiting people by letter alone. Phone
  calls and personal visits generally yield far better
  responses.

Here's what a 1994 study shows for the top reasons people visit a church the first time:

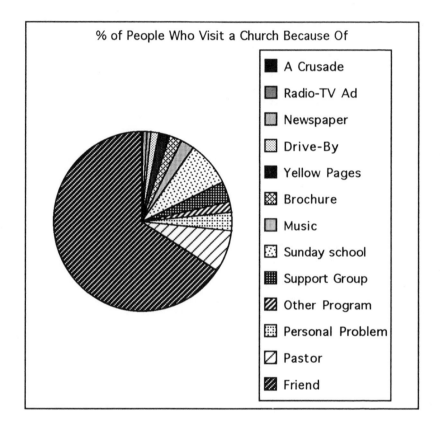

% of People Who Visit a Church Because Of

- A Crusade
- Radio-TV Ad
- Newspaper
- Drive-By
- Yellow Pages
- Brochure
- Music
- Sunday school
- Support Group
- Other Program
- Personal Problem
- Pastor
- Friend

Overcoming Limited Advertising Resources

A few huge churches have the resources to invest large sums of money in advertising and to broadcast their worship services on radio and television. Most churches, however, have relatively little money available for advertising. Thus it becomes extremely important to use those funds as wisely as possible and to seek the least expensive ways of getting word out about the church.

What are the factors which cause people to visit a church worship service or other church program for the first time? While the church certainly has much to learn from marketing agencies and advertising executives, it's crucial to remember that the reasons people come to church are not identical to the reasons for which they choose a particular restaurant, retail store, fitness center, or social service agency. Those who specialize in work with restaurants and retail stores generally list factors such as the following as major influences on consumer choices among existing options:

- Location
- Price
- Name recognition
- Building attractiveness
- Selection
- Quality of service

With the exception of events like weddings, churches generally do not have price or fee scales. The other factors listed, however, do play an important role in the selection of churches by those who are not already members. Some retail specialists insist that the number one, two, and three factors for retail shopping decisions are LOCATION, LOCATION, and LOCATION. There are certainly instances of people driving miles for a superior dining

49

experience at an excellent restaurant or for the opportunity to shop at a store which has a huge selection and low prices; but given the hurried pace of life, location will very often be a key factor.

The chart on page 48 gives the top reasons people gave in a 1994 study for visiting a church the first time. While many factors were involved, the overwhelming reason people came for the first time was because a friend, neighbor, or coworker invited them to come. Certainly word-of-mouth reports on restaurants and stores have a great deal to do with the choices people make, but by no means to the extent that is the case with a local church. Formal studies conducted by all kinds of organizations repeatedly reaffirm that the most influential factor in bringing people to a church is the direct invitation or positive recommendation of others. No other factor is even close in importance.

Some of the data from studies of extremely large congre-gations, some of which are referred to as mega-churches, indicates that commercial advertising may have greater influence on causing people to visit those churches than is the case for most congregations. Since most churches do not spend a large amount of money on advertising, it would probably be unrealistic to expect significant impact from purchased radio, television, or newspaper ads. The experience of many churches, however, which have invested considerable money in advertising on a trial basis continues to be that the purchased ads may help but are still not major influences on bringing people to church. For the most part, what the advertisements seem to accomplish is to increase name recognition so that there is more likely to be a positive response *when a personal invitation to attend worship services or another church event is shared by a friend, neighbor, or coworker.*

Whether your church has generous sums of money with which to work or a very limited budget, the first emphasis should always be on helping existing members invite others to church. This generally involves training programs and perhaps the accompanying purchase of some print and video resources, but those expenditures are very low compared to the purchase of space or time from a newspaper, radio station, or television station. A related expenditure usually should be made for the provision of brochures which describe your church and the programs and services offered. The process of inviting others to your church and of conducting neighborhood canvasses is generally made easier when people are provided with an attractive brochure or other printed information which can be given to potential visitors.

Let's look now at the same data which was given in the pie chart with the factor of friends, neighbors, and coworkers taken out so that the relative influence of the other factors can more easily be examined:

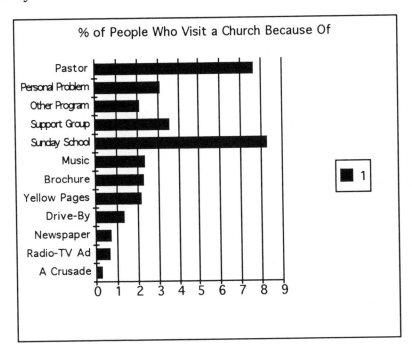

As you look at that information, it's important to remember that these are the responses people listed as the *most* important factors in causing them to visit for the first time. That doesn't mean other factors were not important, and the impact of some of the secondary influences will be considered as we briefly discuss each of the factors:

The Pastor can be a key factor in causing people to visit a church. When people were asked in follow-up interviews why the pastor was given as the most important influence, they were about equally divided between persons who had met the pastor in some situation and people who had heard about the pastor through others. Some people encountered the pastor at a wedding or funeral; some met the pastor in a hospital or nursing home when visiting a friend who was also being seen by the pastor; some met the pastor when he or she personally called on them as a part of visiting homes in a neighborhood; and some met the pastor through a school or community function. People who came because they had heard about the pastor from others generally did so because the pastor had a reputation for being:

- Caring and warm

- Accepting and nonjudgmental

- A good speaker

Certainly the pastor does play a key role in how the church is viewed by the community since he or she is generally the most visible symbol of the church with the exception of the building itself. Members of the church who talk positively about their pastor improve the image of the church and improve the probability of people attending. It's also clear that the quality of the pastor's interaction in a variety of settings may have more influence on the probability of people visiting the church than has often been taken to be the case.

The Sunday School plays even a slightly greater role than the pastor as a means of causing people to visit the church. Here are some of the reasons people shared in interviews for having listed the Sunday school as the top factor in their decision to visit a church:

- The Sunday school having the reputation of offering excellent children's classes.

- The status of people as new parents causing them to be concerned about the spiritual development of their child or children.

- The fact that they had a child in a day care or nursery school program of the church and wanted a similar high-quality experience for their children on Sunday.

- The encouragement their children received from friends who were in Sunday school.

- A personal invitation received to attend an adult class or a social event of an adult class.

- An invitation extended in a canvassing program to attend Vacation Bible School or a rally day.

It's clear, of course, that the influence of friends or neighbors and of the friends of children played an important part in people knowing about the Sunday school and giving consideration to the church because of that. Most of our churches have not maximized the possibilities for outreach through the Sunday school. Aside from printed materials for distribution and sharing, there are almost no financial expenditures involved in outreach through the Sunday school. Some additional curriculum materials may be needed as outreach efforts are successful.

Personal Problems are an inevitable part of life, and their occurrence sometimes draws people to church. The specific nature of the problem, as shared in follow-up interviews, varied greatly from person to person. Examples shared included: the serious illness of a close friend or family member, the death of a close friend or family member, personal illness, depression, suicidal thoughts, alcohol or other drug problems, and strained or broken relationships with spouses or close friends. When asked what caused them to choose a particular church as the one to attend, the most frequent responses were the location, the fact that a friend or family member went there, or the fact that no one they knew went there.

Music is sometimes listed as a reason people choose to visit a particular church. While the reputation of the church for a high quality music program sometimes brought people as visitors to worship services, they were more likely to come because they were invited to sing in a choir, play a musical instrument for a special program, or perform a solo. Thus the music program of the church can be one of the important ways that people reach out to nonmembers.

Support Groups seem to be increasing in importance as a means to draw people as visitors to a church. The influence of this factor in the 1994 study which provided the data for the chart is 75% greater than in a similar 1992 study. Support groups are being offered for people needing encouragement and support because of alcohol problems, other drug problems, single parent status, depression, divorce, the death of a loved one, and other life situations. While the motivation in offering such groups should be that of service to the church and community in Christ's name, one of the practical results will be the support group's becoming a port of entry to the church for at least some people.

Other Programs include small study groups, youth groups, women's groups, men's groups, and retreats. All these activities are possible ports of entry to the church.

Brochures were listed as a primary reason by some people, but the way in which the brochure was received is also important. Most people received brochures as the result of a neighborhood canvass or directly from a friend, neighbor, or coworker. Very few of those persons listing a brochure or other printed information as the reason for coming received the printed material in the mail. While it is true that direct mail efforts can have some impact, that strategy is not nearly as effective as the distribution of printed materials by people.

An increasing number of churches are using direct mail as a strategy, targeting either new residents (obtaining names through commercial mailing list services) or sending to all the people on a particular carrier route (working cooperatively with the Post Office and with a mailing list service). These efforts can bring people to the church, especially when the mailings are of high quality; but it usually takes a series of two, three, or four mailings, spaced closely together in time, to the same people to have significant impact. You have no doubt noticed that you sometimes receive two or more similar offers from the same secular company within a two month period of time. Repeated direct mail tests show that the additional mailings after the first one can significantly increase the percentage of people who respond positively.

To work most effectively, the mailing needs to include not only a brochure, but also a cover letter signed by the pastor or by the pastor and an elected church official. The brochure is what people are most likely to keep and to study, but the letter is more likely than the brochure to gain an immediate reading by the recipient. While the same brochure can be used with more than one mailing to the same person, the content of the letter needs to change. The first letter should be a welcome to the community (for new residents) or an introduction to the church (for carrier routes); the second letter may highlight a particular program or service of potential benefit to the recipient of the letter; and the third letter should highlight the church's concern for the recipient. A fourth letter, if used, can be a variation on the second or third letter.

If your church has word processing capability and can merge the names and addresses into the letter, your response rate will improve considerably over simply using a form letter and a bulk mail approach. The time and expense of the word processing letters with individual signatures and first class postage are generally a worthwhile investment.

Some churches also include a response card with options such as:

_____ I am interested in your church and will attend in the near future.

_____ I would like to have more information about your church; please contact me.

_____ I already have a church home.

_____ Other: _____

The best mailing lists of new residents are those which are limited to persons who have moved a certain minimum distance (such as fifty miles). People who have simply moved from one residence in the community to another residence are not as likely to be looking for a new church home.

One exception to the need for two, three, or four coordinated mailings to the same people comes with the promotion of special emphases such as Easter and Christmas services. Some churches design attractive cards in a size such as 4" X 6" (always check the dimensions with the Post Office before printing) to emphasize a particular service. People who are Christians but not active in a particular church are more likely to be drawn to the church at Easter and Christmas.

Whether your brochure is designed for use on a friend-to-friend basis, in canvassing, or with direct mail, it's important to keep the thrust of the brochure on the needs of the recipient rather than on the programs of the church. When developing copy for a brochure, the natural tendency is to focus on what the church has to offer. While that is important, the main emphasis in the brochure (as with newspaper ads, radio spots, and television spots) should be on the needs of people. Talk about the desire to draw closer to God, the universal concern of parents for the moral and spiritual development of their children, and the desire for a sense of belonging. Show how the worship services, classes, and other programs of your church relate to those needs.

While brochures are not as likely to be listed as a top influence as are friends, pastors, and the Sunday school, they are an important component of most church growth efforts because they provide basic information and may well be kept and studied by potential visitors and prospective members. If money is tight, however, distribute the brochure on a friend-to-friend basis, through neighborhood canvassing, and to visitors at church. Direct mail strategies require considerable investment of funds.

The Yellow Pages are the place new residents are most likely to look for church information if they are seeking a church home on their own. Repeated studies show that people are far more likely to learn about your church through the yellow pages than through the religious page of a local newspaper. Unless you are located in a very small town, you want to be listed in the yellow pages. The percentage of people who list the yellow pages as the top reason for an initial visit may not appear impressive to you, but consider the fact that many people who learn about the church from friends or neighbors nevertheless turn to the yellow pages to look up the address and the times of worship services and Sunday school. Your yellow pages advertisement should include:

- The name of the church, the address, and the phone number. If the street is not well-known, then include a couple of phrases with directions from a better-known, nearby street.

- The times for worship and Christian education.

- Information about child care (if provided).

- Information about wheelchair accessibility if applicable. Many people who are not confined to a wheelchair nevertheless have problems with stairs because of arthritis, heart trouble, respiratory trouble, or other physical conditions.

- If the summer schedule is different, then include that schedule; or if the space for a full summer schedule is too costly, then instruct people to phone the church office for times.

- The name(s) of the minister(s) should be included unless you are in a time of transition.

- If your church has volunteers willing to provide transportation, then include a phone number for people to request that service.

In conjunction with the yellow pages advertisement, think about the best use of the church phone during hours when no one is present to answer calls. Increasing numbers of churches are using answering machines, but the messages on those machines are usually geared to current members more than to prospective members. Have a message on the machine which gives current information on the schedule of services and also tells people where to call if they have an emergency.

The **Drive-By** response was made by persons whose interest in the church had been developed as a result of driving or walking by the physical facilities. While the percentage here is not high, note that it is considerably more likely to draw people than advertisements in newspapers, on radio, or on television. Many persons who responded with other factors as the top reason for a visit also identified the location and appearance of the church itself as a secondary factor. Those who actually visit will obviously evaluate the church in part on the basis of outward appearances. These realities mean that the building needs to be in good condition, the lawn needs to be attractive, and there needs to be a good sign which can easily be read from the street.

Less than 1% of those who visit do so primarily because of **Newspaper** advertising or information. In most communities, regular newspaper advertising is expensive and will not generally be worth the investment. Larger churches which can afford larger advertisements will gain more than small and medium sized churches with little money to devote to this strategy. These guidelines may be of help in thinking about newspaper publicity:

* By all means accept any free listings which are available. Merchants sometimes cooperatively sponsor a listing of church services.

* If you use paid advertising, you can increase the effectiveness by:
  - Placing the ad on the sports page or the features page rather than the religious page so the unchurched will see it.
  - Focusing the ad copy on the needs of people more than on the offerings of the church.
  - Including a picture of the church or the pastor in the ad, if the cost is not prohibitive.

* By all means, do frequent news releases about programs in your church which may be of interest to the public. Those news stories involve no cost to your congregation and may catch the interest of prospective members. Find out from the paper the form in which it likes to receive news releases. The better written and easier to edit your news release is, the greater the probability of its use.

Radio and Television do not seem to have significant impact on drawing people to the church. That remains true not only in terms of being the primary draw for a first visit but also in terms of secondary impact. Some persons who specialize in radio and television advertising openly acknowledge that people are not overly influenced on church decisions by what is said on radio or television. Others will argue, perhaps correctly, that impact from radio and television advertising comes over a fairly substantial period of time and requires significant investment. Since most churches do not have the resources to make that investment, it's not surprising that so few have positive results to report. Here are some of the things that seem to work best:

- Some of the excellent human interest spots
  developed by denominational agencies are
  very positively received by the public and do
  contribute to a positive image of the denomination
  itself and of the sponsoring local church.

- Short spots which relate the programs of the
  local church *directly to* the needs of listeners
  or viewers are far more effective than spots
  which simply emphasize the quality of what
  the church offers.

- The broadcast of worship services can be a
  valuable service for persons confined to hospitals,
  nursing homes, or their own residences. Their
  broadcast, however, does not generally draw people
  to the church. Most of those who watch such
  services do so because they are unable to attend
  services in a local church - and the majority of
  the audience will be people who already are connected with the church doing the broadcasting.
  High quality broadcasting, like that done by Robert
  Schuller, requires substantial investment in state-
  of-the-art equipment and an arrangement of the
  service for the convenience and interest of the
  television audience.

Community access channels on cable television provide
another means for church involvement in the media. Many
cable stations need community involvement in programming and
will be cooperative and helpful with churches which wish to do
programming. The preference of the cable channels, of course, is
for programs which have reasonably broad community interest
rather than for broadcasts of worship services. Such
programming will not necessarily be a primary draw in getting
prospective members to your church, but quality programming
can be a service to the community, a good creative outlet for
some people in your church, and part of building a positive
image of the church in the community. I've provided some
suggestions for cable programming in the book *Reaching Out
Through Christian Education* (available from The Andrew Center).

Crusades do not appear to play as major a role in winning
new people to Christ or interesting people in the local church as

was once the case. There are exceptions, of course, especially when one considers the ministries of Billy Graham and Luis Palau. For the most part, however, crusades are not the draw they were in times past. There are any number of reasons for this reality including the chaotic schedules of people, the impact of television, and the impact of recent religious scandals.

There are parts of the country, however, in which crusades and revivals still do have influence and the potential for outreach. The results of a given crusade or revival generally depend in good measure on the amount of preparatory work done by the church or churches sponsoring the event. With lots of publicity and person-to-person encouragement of attendance, it isn't necessary to have a nationally known speaker in order to draw a crowd to a crusade or revival.

Some local churches like to have revivals or renewal services for the purpose of renewing the faith and enthusiasm of those who are already members. These churches are not primarily concerned about reaching the unchurched through a revival, but recognize considerable benefit that can come through new commitment on the part of existing members. With an appropriate emphasis on church members inviting friends who do not have a church home, it's still possible for these events to reach beyond the sponsoring congregation(s).

Do be sure that you have full knowledge of the financial practices and requirements of any individual or organization with whom you enter into a relationship for a crusade or revival. If your denomination has an approved list of such individuals and organizations, that may be the most reliable source from which to make your selection. In terms of national, nondenominational organizations, this author has had the most positive experiences in connection with crusades conducted by Billy Graham's organization (which has a number of associate evangelists who are available for work in many different communities). That organization works in close cooperation with local churches and recognizes the importance of persons who make new commitments to Christ being immediately plugged into the life of a local congregation. Staff people with the Graham organization are also open and honest about the handling of expenses and offerings.

Another Look at Entry Points

When we identify strategies to get prospective members to church, we understandably focus primarily on ways to invite them to attend worship services. Yet as the chart in the previous chapter shows, many people are first drawn to church because of the Sunday school, support groups, music groups, or other program opportunities. All of these may be seen as "ports of entry" or "entry points" to the life of the church. If people start attending any one of the groups or programs of the church, then there is a greatly improved probability that they will attend other services and events and eventually become members. Focusing only on inviting people to worship services may be a barrier to church growth because we are narrowing the potential number of ports of entry to a single option.

Most rapidly growing churches have learned to utilize as many different entry points as possible and to encourage those who work with all the groups and programs of the church to be alert for opportunities to involve people who are not yet members. One of the motivations for developing new programs in the church is to make available as many entry points as possible, relative to the size of the congregation. Consider the following as possible entry points:

- Sunday school classes. Many Sunday schools develop aggressive outreach programs which involve students of almost all ages in inviting their friends and neighbors to share in Sunday school activities.

- Sunday school class social events. Many adult classes have a tradition of meeting once a month on a social basis - sometimes at the home of a member, sometimes at the church, and sometimes at a restaurant, park, or movie theater. These social occasions provide ideal opportunities for class members to invite friends, especially those who might feel more threatened if asked to attend an actual class on a Sunday morning. The social event lets them meet others in the class and develop some relationships, which can pave the way to a desire to be more fully involved.

• Nursery school and day care programs can be of great value as entry points. With increasing numbers of households with both parents working or with single parents, the need for nursery school and day care is enormous in virtually every community. If a church offers high quality child care services, that may well draw people into the overall life of the church. It's important for those who work with the nursery school or day care program to be intentional about inviting parents to other church activities. Many nursery schools and day care centers have found that offering seminars on topics like "Parenting Young Children," "The Spiritual Life of Children," or "Raising a Child Safely in a Dangerous World" can draw a large percentage of parents. The pastor or other staff members can be involved in the seminar. (This strategy will not work as well if the nursery school or day care center is not an official program of the church. It's also important to respect the fact that some parents will already have another church home.)

• Weddings provide an opportunity for the pastor and the church to develop a relationship with some persons who are not members of the congregation. As discussed in my report *Fifty Ways to Reach Young Singles, Couples, and Families*, some churches should consider modifying their fee structure for nonmember weddings in a way that encourages participation in the church. Instead of asking couples to pay for the use of the sanctuary and the reception hall, ask them to attend, for example, six worship services and six Sunday school classes. Whether or not they keep coming will depend in good measure on how well the people of the church respond to their presence.

- Music programs offer many opportunities to reach out to others. Members of the choir and of other musical groups can invite friends, neighbors, or coworkers with musical interest and skill to participate. Some choirs do significant outreach to the community by performing at hospitals, nursing homes, jails, shopping malls, and parks. All those performances present the church in a positive light and have the possibility of reaching new people.

- Children's choirs and youth choirs merit special mention because they can be such valuable entry points, initially for the children and youth who want opportunities to sing but eventually for their parents as well, who become interested in the church through their children's involvement. As many public schools continue to cut back on funding for music and art, church choirs become an increasingly important opportunity for children and young people. Some youth choirs go on tour in the summer, making them especially attractive.

- The youth program of the church can be an excellent entry point for young people without a church home. They start attending the youth group because of the invitation of another young person and then continue attending because of the relationships which develop. The teens in your present youth group can be effective in reaching out to their peers. (This is discussed more fully in the book *Peer Evangelism*, which was written by myself and Sam Detwiler.)

- Support groups, as discussed in the last chapter, are a worthwhile service to the church and the community. Persons who do not have a church home and become involved in a support group sponsored by your congregation may in time become interested in other aspects of your church.

- Bible study groups and other small group experiences can also be valuable entry points to your church. When these groups are held in the homes of members, it becomes especially easy for those who are attending to invite their friends and neighbors to participate. People who are inclined to be suspicious of the church will be considerably less threatened by an invitation to be part of a group which meets in a private home or apartment. If they have a positive experience in the group and form relationships with others from the congregation, they are far more likely to be interested later in worship services and in church membership.

- Some local churches have begun contemporary worship services as new entry points to the church for persons who have negative feelings about more traditional worship services. While the tendency in most churches has been to offer these services on a Thursday, Friday, or Saturday evening, that may not always be the best approach. Many of those who are not active in the church are actually more likely to be free on Sunday morning than on any evening. Most churches also find it easier to recruit volunteer staffing for a new service on Sunday morning because people are already present for the traditional service and for Sunday school. The barrier to Sunday morning is often the difficulty of adding a worship service without causing disruption in the schedule of existing activities. With large numbers of people, especially in the young adult years, turned off by traditional music and sermons, contemporary services can be a helpful part of a church growth strategy in some communities. Most successful contemporary services come about *after* a substantial period of surveying present members and potential members and *after* involving a large number of persons in the planning process. (The more people involved in the planning process, the greater the probability that the service will begin with a good crowd!)

- Special programs in the church can also be entry points. The range of possibilities is enormous:

    - Ice cream socials

    - Chili suppers

    - Breakfast with the bunny (an Easter season event described in my book *Fifty Ways to Reach Young Singles, Couples, and Families*)

    - Chocolate tasting fairs

    - Nonviolent toy fairs (a Christmas season event)

    - Spiritual growth seminars

    - Marriage enrichment seminars or retreats

    - Seminars focused on community problems such as drugs, violence, or teen pregnancy

    With any special event or program, your church needs to have a registration process which generates the names, addresses, and phone numbers of those who attend. You may even wish to include a section on the registration form which lets people indicate membership status:

    ___ Member of this church
    ___ Member of another church
    ___ Not a church member

- Women's groups and men's groups can be good entry points, even though these organizations are in many places not as popular as in some previous decades.

- Senior citizen groups are increasingly important as most communities continue to experience significant growth in the number of persons who are retired or who are of retirement age. With all the focus on young adults in our churches, it's important not to forget the needs of senior

citizens who constitute a large percentage of
the church and the community.

- Young adult groups of many kinds can be
valuable entry points. Many young adults who
have reservations about the institutional church
are far more likely to come to a social group than
to worship services or a Sunday school class.
They don't fear being caught in a discussion of
religious dogma or being asked for a commitment
to the church when in a social setting. The social
setting lets visitors form bonds with those who are
active in the church and can help them, in time,
be more comfortable with involvement in the church.
Friday night supper clubs have become increasingly
popular with young singles.

With creative thinking, you can identify additional existing
entry points for your church and generate ideas for new groups
or programs which could help bring people into positive contact
with your church. In planning for any of these, be sure that you
have a system in place to get the names and addresses of those
who participate and to follow up on those persons with
invitations to other church activities.

Overcoming Inadequate Visitor Follow-Up

Many of the potential barriers discussed thus far have been related to getting people to a point of initial contact with the church through visiting a worship service or Sunday school class, participating in a social group, or attending a special event or program. Obviously no one is going to be interested in becoming a member of the church unless that person first begins to participate in activities of the church. Getting them to attend, however, is just the beginning. Some churches put so much energy into bringing people into an initial contact with the church that they have none left for the crucial follow-up to keep people coming and eventually bring them into membership.

Follow-Up Begins at the Time of the Visit

What happens from the time the visitor first approaches the church will have a great deal to do with the probability of that person eventually becoming a member. It's important for parking to be clearly marked (some churches even reserve spaces for visitors), and for there to be a greeter at each entrance to the church. The greeter should be prepared not only to extend a warm welcome, but also to help with directions to Sunday school classes, the sanctuary, and the restrooms.

Members of Sunday school classes should be prepared to make the guest feel welcome and to see that several introductions get made. Those responsible for the Sunday school class should not assume that the visitor will automatically attend worship services unless that person clearly states that he or she has already done so or intends to do so following the class. As a result, the name and address of the visitor should be conveyed to the church office and to whatever group has the overall responsibility for responding to visitors. Classes which have not already done so should develop a registration card or form to make it easy to obtain that information, though skilled leaders can also get it in the process of conversation with the visitor.

Many churches have for years assumed that anyone who attends a worship service wants to be introduced to the whole congregation. Several recent studies have shown, however, that about two-thirds of those who visit a worship service for the first time feel embarrassed if introduced to the whole congregation. Because of that reality, increasing numbers of churches are not putting people on the spot in front of the whole congregation. Some churches have an informal greeting and mixing time at the beginning or middle of the worship service when people mingle to greet others and make introductions. When that is practiced, the visitor is able to meet several people without feeling singled out.

Coffee or fellowship times have become increasingly common on Sunday morning either before or after the service(s) of worship. These provide another opportunity for informal introductions of visitors to be made. Many churches have volunteers who function as hosts or hostesses during the fellowship time. They are on the lookout for visitors and see that those persons are made to feel welcome and are introduced to some other people.

Name tags are becoming more popular in churches because of the difficulty even long-term members may have in knowing all the members of the church. Members sometimes fail to greet visitors out of fear that they may in fact be greeting someone who has been a member for years. When all members have name tags which have been prepared on a typewriter or computer, then it's much easier to identify visitors, for whom tags are usually made with markers by a greeter.

Churches which are especially focused on reaching young singles sometimes have a standing group of people who go out together for brunch on Sunday. If those persons are alert, they can extend an invitation to any single persons who are visiting to join them for brunch. There are also instances in which couples or families who meet visitors and realize that they have no brunch plans issue an invitation. It's important to be sensitive to the personality of the visitors. Some visitors are clearly open to and appreciative of that kind of invitation, but it can be threatening to others. Training should make it clear that, when in doubt, it's better to delay a Sunday before issuing a brunch invitation.

The procedures used when people have their first contact at a small group, a choir rehearsal, or another mid-week or evening meeting are similar to those used in Sunday school classes with one exception - the presence of a person at an activity other than a worship service or Sunday school class should not be taken as a clear indicator of that person's interest in membership.

When the first contact is in that kind of setting, the interest may be more tentative; and it becomes important not to push too quickly. The person extending the original invitation to attend, the leader of the group, or another person in the group should take the responsibility for visiting informally with that person and determining at what point in time it becomes appropriate to extend an invitation to a worship service or to arrange for a home visit by a lay volunteer or a staff member. Each group should have a procedure to ensure that visitors are not overlooked. In most instances, the leader of the group should designate a group member to maintain that contact unless the identity of the person extending the original invitation is clearly known.

Names and addresses of visitors to mid-week and evening groups should be shared with the church office or with another central clearing house, but along with the name and address should be a clear notation of whether or not it is appropriate yet for there to be other contacts. When that person does appear at a worship service or a Sunday school class, that information should be shared back with the group that had the first contact with the prospective member.

Follow-Up after the Visit to Worship or Sunday School

The presence of an adult at a worship service or Sunday school class often means that there is potential interest in joining the church. There are, of course, instances when someone who visits a worship service or class is a resident of another community on vacation, is attending because a friend or relative is participating in the service or class, or is interested in what your church is doing but is already actively involved in another congregation. The address given on a registration pad and information obtained through informal visiting before or after the service will often clear up the status of a visitor. Unless you are absolutely certain that the visitor is not a prospective member, it's important to follow through on the attendance on the assumption that he or she could be.

Repeated studies have made it clear that prompt follow-up on a visitor to worship or Sunday school class makes a tremendous difference in the probability of that person returning and eventually becoming a member. Most rapidly growing churches follow up the attendance with a visit to the person's home within twenty-four to forty-eight hours.

Contrast that with the habit many churches have of simply mailing a letter from the pastor to the visitor. While letters done by today's computer and word processing equipment are at least more personal than the form letters of the past, this kind of response is very inadequate. There's nothing wrong with sending a letter, but that shouldn't be the only response to a visit - except in those instances when the person clearly was simply on vacation or when the person was clearly attending because of a relationship with someone in your congregation and is already known to have a church home.

The following chart shows the results of one study which was conducted in churches of the Assemblies of God, United Methodist, American Baptist, Evangelical Lutheran, United Church of Christ, and Disciples of Christ denominations during 1993. As the chart clearly shows, the kind of response chosen to the initial attendance of a person at a worship service was directly related to the probability of that person attending a second time. Those who received a visit in the home which included the delivery of baked goods were by some measure the most likely to return. A visit without the baked goods was reasonably effective. Note that the difference between sending a form letter and doing nothing was not significant.

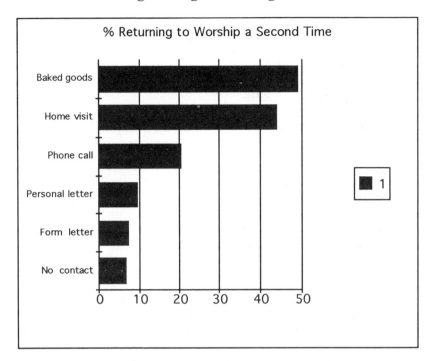

The visit within the first day or two after attendance does not have to be lengthy and can be made by a staff member or by a lay volunteer. In most instances, the visit will be most effective if made by a lay volunteer because that shows clear interest in the person as an individual but does not communicate the kind of pressure that some people feel from the presence of the pastor or another staff member.

Volunteers generally find the visit an easier one to make if they have something to take: freshly baked cookies or bread and informational literature about the church are a good combination. All the volunteer has to do is communicate appreciation for the person attending the service or class and then share the baked goods and literature. If the person being visited takes the initiative for a longer conversation or has questions, then the volunteer can proceed to share more information about the church and may be able to learn more about the person. In some instances, the volunteer may decide that it's appropriate to take additional steps such as:

- Asking the pastor or another church staff member to call on the prospective member.

- Asking a representative of a Sunday school class or a social group to extend an invitation to the prospective member.

- Asking the choir director or another program person to extend an invitation to involvement.

- Extend a personal invitation or suggest that another person extend an invitation to the individual or family for brunch on the following Sunday.

If the congregation is doing a good job of friend-to-friend inviting or witnessing, it is quite possible that the visitor will have come because of contact already made by another member of the church. In those instances, that person should generally be the one to follow through on seeing that the prospective member becomes more fully involved in the life of the church. Even when that is the case, however, it's good for a different person to take baked goods and literature to that visitor. That's a caring act which shows that the warmth of the church is not limited to the person who extended the original invitation.

When an individual or family attends an additional one or two services or classes, the church should take that as a clear sign that this individual or family should be cultivated for membership. At that point it becomes important to assign the care and nurturing of the potential member(s) to a specific individual or couple in the church. As already discussed, when it is known that a specific person extended the original invitation, then that person is probably the one who should follow through. If that is not the case, then an assignment should be made. Churches have used a variety of titles for the individual who maintains the major contact with the prospective member - "faith friend" is one of the most commonly used and will be used in the remainder of this book to designate that relationship.

Following the first visit made to the home of the prospective member, the exact pace at which contact should proceed has to be determined on an individual basis by the person accepting the faith friend responsibility. Some people who are prospective members have been involved in a church all of their lives and are ready to become involved in many phases of the church. These persons often want to become members quickly, and the church should respond with enthusiasm to that interest. There are other persons, however, who are considerably more reserved and who may be having their first contact ever with a local church. These persons will spook if they feel the church is pushing too hard. They need low key, laid back contact which affirms their importance to the church but which puts them under no pressure.

The pastor and other staff people need to be involved at some point in the process, but the exact timing depends on the staff workload of the church and the needs of the prospective member as identified by the faith friend. Certainly within the first month of attendance, there should be a staff contact.

There needs to be a clear flow of information between the faith friend and the staff of the church, so that the pastor or other staff stay aware of the status of the prospective member and of what needs to be done. As indicated earlier in this chapter, the church office or a volunteer needs to serve as a clearing house for all information about prospective members.

Visitors to Special Events

The first contact of people with the church will sometimes come through their attendance at a one-time event such as a dinner, a seminar, or another special program - see the examples in the chapter on entry points. It's crucial to have a registration process for these events if any meaningful follow-up is to be done. That form should provide an optional place for persons to indicate the status of their church affiliation. Most people will complete that information, and it helps the church immediately determine whether any further steps should be taken.

A group of persons who serve as a clearing house for information on prospective members or who have accepted responsibility for follow-up on special events should go through the registrations. Those persons who are already members of your church or of another church in the community should not be considered prospective members.

The follow-up on persons who do not have a church home should be done with sensitivity to the reality that their attendance at a special event does not mean they are interested in church membership. If they were seriously interested in church membership, they would probably have shown up at a worship service or Sunday school class in the past. Having a positive experience at the special event will occasionally motivate someone to try a worship service or Sunday school class, but some gentle encouragement is generally needed if that is to happen. There are several strategies which can be used:

- Follow up the special event attendance with a letter thanking them for their participation and extending an invitation to them to attend worship services or Sunday school if they wish to do so. A brochure about the church can be enclosed with the letter.

- Follow up the special event attendance by having a volunteer make a phone call thanking that person for participation and extending an invitation to attend worship services or Sunday school classes. If the person attending has children, a special emphasis might be placed on Sunday school opportunities.

- Follow up the special event attendance by having a volunteer make a brief visit to the home for the purpose of sharing a brochure about the church and extending an invitation to attend worship services and Sunday school.

- Follow up the special event attendance with an invitation to participate in another event, class, or program which is related to the same theme or issue. The invitation can be extended by letter, phone call, or personal visit. This approach is often ideal because it offers a specific invitation in line with the interest the person has already shown. For example:

  - If someone has attended a breakfast with the bunny event before Easter or a non-violent toy fair before Christmas, extend an invitation to a seminar on "Developing the Spiritual Life of Children."

- If someone has attended a seminar on parenting teenagers and an adult Sunday school class is about to begin a unit on understanding young people, extend an invitation to attend that class.

- If someone has attended a special concert at the church and the music is similar to what is featured at a contemporary worship service, invite the person to share in that service.

The Clearing House Function

Because there are many potential entry points to the church, it's important for the church office or a volunteer to maintain careful records about all visitors to any events. Some churches do this through a system of notecards; others do it on computer. The information maintained should include:

- The name, address, and phone number of the person.

- What the initial contact was and who reported that contact.

- What follow-up was made to the initial contact (Sam Davis delivered a plate of cookies and asked Betty Ford to invite the couple to her Sunday school class).

- What the next contact was and who reported that.

- Regular updates on what happens in the development of that person's relationship with the church.

If the first contact of people is at a worship service or a Sunday school class, then they should normally be placed on the mailing list for the church newsletter. The newsletter is generally not appropriate for those whose first contact is through another entry point in the church, unless the person reporting the attendance suggests that the newsletter would be appreciated. It's also important to have a system for removing names from the newsletter list if two or three months pass without the person attending again.

In a large congregation, the church office or the volunteer who serves as the clearing house may need to be supplemented by a small committee or task force which meets frequently to review the progress on member recruitment. It's important to see that information gets relayed to anyone having contact with the potential member. Suppose, for example, that a person attends a small group meeting in a home and that the leader of the small group reports the contact to the clearing house. If the prospective member attends a worship service, then the small group leader needs to be notified, since the worship attendance indicates an increased level of interest in the church.

Another example would be a person who attended a worship service in May, responded appreciatively to the delivery of baked goods, but then did not return to worship again until August. That person should again receive a brief visit and baked goods, but it's important for the person making the visit to know that this person also attended in May. By knowing about the prior attendance, the person delivering the baked goods may be able to visit for a few minutes and learn something more about the extent of the person's interest in the church.

Overcoming
Difficult Assimilation

In order for the church to effectively involve new people as members, three things must happen:

1. People must become interested enough in the church to start attending.

2. People must become involved enough in the church to want to belong.

3. People must become invested enough in the church to continue as active members.

One of the great frustrations many churches experience is that they are successful with the first two steps but fail at the third. If people only join the church to become inactive members, then no one gains anything. The new members certainly do not gain if they no longer derive benefit from involvement. The church certainly does not gain since most congregations already have all the inactive members needed!

A 1993-1994 study has taken a careful look at the reasons people give for dropping out of church activity within the first two years following their acceptance into formal membership. The chart on the next page shows the factors which were shared as the top reasons for not continuing to be involved. These should provide good perspective on what needs to be done to prevent people from dropping out.

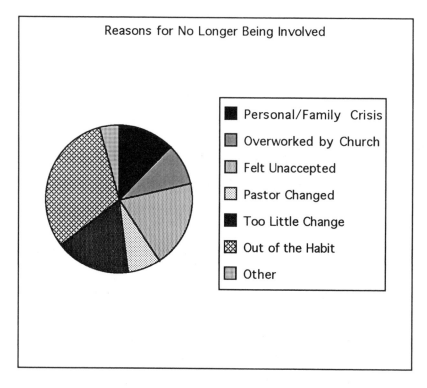

Reasons for No Longer Being Involved

- Personal/Family Crisis
- Overworked by Church
- Felt Unaccepted
- Pastor Changed
- Too Little Change
- Out of the Habit
- Other

The single reason most frequently given, by 31.5% of those who responded, was that people simply got **out of the habit**. Obviously there may in some instances have been deeper reasons which people were less comfortable sharing; but it also has to be recognized that the habits of regular attendance and financial giving are easily broken - even by persons who have been church members for many years. Once the initial enthusiasm of involvement in the church has passed, new members are not likely to continue those habits unless they feel a part of the overall life of the church and believe that their participation is important to the church.

Other studies have indicated that prompt follow-up on breaks in regular attendance patterns at worship and Sunday school in many cases results in persons returning to regular activity. If people are simply out of the habit, then the contact reminds them that they are important to the church and helps them establish the involvement again before they have been gone so long that it feels awkward to return. The contact needs to be made within one to six weeks of the initial break in attendance pattern in order to be effective, and the earlier the better!

The second most frequent reason, given by 19%, was that the new members **felt unaccepted** in the church. When given space for comments, several respondents wrote that they had at first felt warmly welcomed by members of the church, but that with the passage of time they felt that they were not really wanted, or at least not wanted for anything other than their financial contributions. They took as indicators that they were not wanted such instances as:

- People who were long-time members introducing themselves again and again - obviously not learning the names of the new members, though the new members were learning the names of the long-time members.

- The church failing to ask them to serve on a board, committee, or task force. They were also not often asked to be ushers or greeters. They were most likely to be asked to teach children's classes, since that was the primary area of recruitment difficulty in most of the churches in the study.

- Discovering that there were various informal groups within the membership who did things together socially without inviting newer members in similar life situations to join them.

- The fact that it was so often assumed that they would know what long-time members were talking about in adult Sunday school classes and on other occasions - and were made to feel foolish if they acknowledged that they did not.

- The fact that their ideas for improving the life of the church were almost never taken seriously by anyone except the pastor and other new members.

The third most frequently shared reason, by 16.5% of those responding, was that there had been **too little change** in the church. Most of those sharing this as a primary reason were persons who dropped out in the second year of church membership rather than in the first year. These are persons who were attracted to the church by the presence of a sense of excitement and openness to change. Several of these persons identified specific things which had been concerns when they joined the church but which the pastor and others had said should be changed or improved in the future. Some of the things shared which had been desired but did not happen are listed here:

- More young adults in positions of leadership.

- A remodeled youth room and more activities for teenagers.

- The addition of a more contemporary worship service.

- An outreach effort to those of other races living near the church.

- New and significantly improved nursery facilities.

- A social group for young singles.

- A social group for young couples.

The fourth most frequently given reason, by 12.5% of those responding, was that they had experienced a **personal or family crisis** which had caused them to feel uncomfortable in church or to get out of the habit of attending church. The kinds of crises identified included:

- The loss of employment (and the accompanying loss of the ability to pay the pledge made to the church).

- Marital separation or divorce.

- The death of a parent or other family member.

- Serious illness.

- Depression.

- Alcohol or other drug problems.

- Difficulties with children.

Almost all the persons in this category still reflected feeling good about the church and were saddened that they had become inactive. A few of them did express disappointment that they had stopped coming and that no one from the church ever asked why. It was not uncommon for a letter reminding them that their pledge was not current to be the only communication from the church.

Regular follow-up on those persons once they broke a pattern of regular attendance could well have identified the problem being experienced and have provided opportunity for the church to express concern. In most of these instances, that opportunity was lost.

While feeling unaccepted by long-time church members and being frustrated by the slow pace of change in the congregation were reasons for the loss of involvement by many respondents, about 9% of those surveyed felt they had become **overworked by the church**. These persons had become trapped in a higher level of involvement than they wanted! The persons indicating this response, like most of those who fell into inactivity because of the slow pace of change, were most likely to have been regular in attendance during the first year of membership and to have fallen into inactivity sometime during the second year.

Those who felt overworked were most commonly persons who had joined small churches, though some in medium and large sized churches experienced the same problem. In contrast to the churches which made new members feel shut out, most of these churches were so hungry for fresh leadership and inno- vative ideas that they involved the new members everywhere they could. At first this was an extremely positive experience for the new members and reinforced their good feelings about the apparent openness of the congregation. In time, however, they began to feel overworked, taken advantage of, and not fully appreciated.

A significant minority of those who had become inactive,

7.4%, apparently joined the church primarily because of the personal interest of the pastor. When the **pastor changed**, they stopped coming. In some instances, the pastor was in significant conflict with the congregation; and the new members had sided with the pastor. With the pastor leaving, the feelings of the new members for the church changed.

In other instances, the pastor had a good relationship with the congregation and left because of a promotional opportunity or for other personal reasons. The pastor's departure didn't leave the new members feeling hostile toward the church but did result in their becoming more apathetic and made it easier for them to fall out of the habit of regular attendance and involvement.

While it's easy to criticize the pastors in these instances for failing to see that the new members were helped to grow into close relationships with other persons in the church, it's important to remember that such a process does take time. The initial visit to the church by a prospective member will generally come because of an invitation given by someone already in the church - sometimes that person will be the pastor. Once a person begins attending, it becomes the responsibility of everyone in the church to see that the new person feels accepted and included.

The remaining responses on the main reason for no longer being involved in the church, 4.1% of the total, included a wide variety of explanations such as: changes in hours at work making it difficult to attend worship or meetings, changes in child custody arrangements for persons who were divorced with a resulting change in schedule, the conviction that the pastor's sermons were not as good as in the past, and the personal inability to stay involved with a single organization for a long period of time.

In view of this kind of information, what can the local church do to improve the process of assimilation of new members? Several specific strategies seem clear:

1. Membership classes need to help prospective members better understand the church as a whole, including the process by which decisions are made. There are many different opinions about the relative merits of having membership classes which continue for months or of having classes which continue for only a few weeks. I've not seen enough actual data on the relationship between the length of membership preparation classes and the continuing involvement of new members to be willing to argue either side of that debate. Those churches which start requiring attendance at membership classes over a long period of time feel that is better than the short-running classes they used to have. Those churches which have moved from an instructional process that last for months to one which involves only a few weeks seem to feel better with the shorter, more concentrated period of time. In general, churches which *change* their membership class and orientation process seem to feel more enthusiastic about the new process than the old process. In both instances, it appears that the process of evaluating the membership preparation process is a healthy one which brings new enthusiasm and commitment on the part of those providing leadership.

What was clearly missing from the membership class process for most of the persons interviewed in connection with the study discussed earlier in this chapter was information about:

- How decisions are actually made in the church.

- What the process is by which one becomes a part of the church's organizational structure.

- How one should go about sharing a concern or idea for the improvement of the church.

- What is distinctive about the faith tradition of the church.

2. The "faith friend" or a mentor needs to maintain regular contact with the new member for at least one year. In some churches, it's common to think of the responsibility of the "faith friend" ending when the prospective member actually joins the church. The acceptance of formal membership, however, is only one step along the way to true assimilation in the church. It's very important to have an individual who takes personal interest in what continues to happen for the individual, couple, or family who have joined the congregation. If the responsibilities of the faith friend are thought to end at the time of formal membership, then a sponsor or mentor needs to be assigned to the new member. This person can offer regular contact with the new member, answer questions, make introductions to others in the church, and follow up quickly if there is a break in the attendance pattern. That relationship should continue for at least a full year after formal membership has been accepted - and perhaps should continue for two years unless there is a shepherding or pastoral care group to whom responsibility for the new member can be assigned.

3. There need to be frequent efforts to integrate newer and older members of the congregation. Some of this can take place in the membership class itself with key leaders of the church being asked to help present information to the class.

Several churches have experimented very successfully with social events that intentionally mix newer and older members. These often take place in a private home and involve between six and twenty people at a time, depending on the size of the home and the schedules of the people involved. Newer and older members gain the opportunity to visit informally at more depth than is possible during conversations before or after worship services. The response to these events is almost universally positive and results in older members feeling more secure about the commitment and quality of newer members and in newer members gaining appreciation for older members and the heritage of the church. A wise church will structure several such events each year so that all new members and a significant number of older members can take part.

4. New members should be asked for clear commitments to the church. While the ideal length of time for the membership preparation class may be a legitimate topic of debate, there's no question but that commitment needs to be expected from new members. Those joining the congregation should be asked to:

- attend worship and Sunday school on a weekly basis.

- involve any children or youth they have in the life of the church.

- make a pledge (if appropriate in your tradition) and do regular financial giving to the church.

- select one area for ministry and service through the church. The range of possibilities here is large: being a member of a board or committee, teaching or helping with a Sunday school class, advising a youth group, ushering, singing in the choir, helping recruit new members, working with a church sponsored soup kitchen, maintaining bulletin boards, or helping with child care.

5. The congregation should have a clear procedure for responding to persons (whether older or newer members) who break a pattern of regular attendance at worship or Sunday school. Every church needs to have a group of people who are responsible for the continuing care of church members. This group should see that attendance is carefully monitored and that a prompt response is made when people stop attending.

The initial response should generally be by telephone. Letters or cards are not as effective as a phone call, and they may also be interpreted as being critical of the person who has been absent. A phone call can more readily convey that the person was missed and that the caller simply wants to know if there is any problem with which the church may be of help. If it's just a matter of the person having gotten out of the habit for a couple of weeks, the call will generally be sufficient to bring a return to regular attendance. If illness, family problems, or another specific difficulty is shared, then the caller can respond personally or arrange for a response by the pastor if that is more appropriate.

Should the reason for the break in the attendance pattern be that the person feels unaccepted in the church or is frustrated with the slowness of the church to change, that may not necessarily be revealed in response to the phone call. That's why it becomes important for a visit to be made in that person's home if the break in attendance continues. A face-to-face discussion makes it easier to communicate genuine warmth and concern to the nonattending member and creates a climate in which problems are more readily discussed.

One church, which has a program of shepherds who are responsible for the well-being of the membership, adopted the following strategy for dealing with breaks in attendance patterns:

- If a person misses worship services two weeks in a row without an explanation (such as sickness or vacation) being known, then the shepherd for that person should make a telephone contact.

- If a person misses Sunday school two weeks in a row without an explanation being known, then the class teacher should make a telephone contact and also communicate the response to the shepherd.

- If a person misses worship or Sunday school four weeks in a row, the shepherd should go to that person's home for a visit to determine if anything is wrong to which the church should respond.

- The shepherd or the Sunday school teacher will contact the pastor if the phone call or the personal visit reveals a situation to which the pastor should respond - especially illness or the death of a family member.

- The purpose of all contacts with the person who has stopped the pattern of regular attendance should be to reinforce that individual's importance to the church and to seek ways to be of service to that person. At no time should the person who has stopped attending be made to feel that the concern is for the church as an institution rather than for the individual.

6. The nominating committee, gifts discernment committee, or other organization responsible for placing people in positions in the church needs to function throughout the year. Most of our churches are tied into a system in which board members, committee or commission members, and officers are elected or selected once a year. Teachers are also selected once a year - generally at a different time than when other positions are filled.

New members who have enthusiasm and energy shouldn't be forced to wait for several months before being involved in the ministry of the church. There should be some boards and committees to which members can be added at any time, and it should also be possible to have people join a teaching or youth ministry team at any time during the year. Limiting these changes to an annual basis delays new members being able to have the highest possible involvement and also delays their becoming acquainted with the other persons who are working on behalf of the church.

7. Consider the possibility of using a spiritual gifts discernment process as part of the orientation of new members to the church. This kind of process has been referred to earlier in this book, and some organizations with resources which can help are shared on page 26. Helping people become aware of their spiritual gifts and of ways to apply those in the service of the church can generate much deeper excitement and enthusiasm than having them wait until a future time to be asked to take a more active role in the church. A spiritual gifts program starts with the gifts and abilities of the person rather than with the needs of the church. That isn't to say that the needs of the church are without importance but simply that starting with the individual is the best way to keep all people meaningfully involved.

8. The discussion of strategies for improving assimilation into the church has, thus far, focused primarily on adult members; but most of the same strategies are effective with children and youth. Teachers and youth group advisors, especially, need to see that new class or group members get acquainted with others, have opportunities to share their opinions, and are helped to feel part of the class or group. When there is a break in attendance pattern, there should be the same kind of prompt response which was discussed earlier in this chapter.

9. Name tags can be helpful to both older members and newer members. As discussed in an earlier chapter, the use of name tags can save embarrassment for everyone involved. People do need to work at truly *learning* names rather than just reading name tags, but learning names does take time.

10. Churches need volunteers on Sunday morning who see that visitors and new members get introduced to older members of the congregation. With the tendency of many people to feel slightly shy and awkward about meeting strangers, most churches have found value in having a few volunteers who make it their business to identify visitors and new members and to help them mix with others. This system sometimes works best if the volunteers do not have a "job title" and in fact function without telling anyone that they have specifically been asked to perform the mixing and introducing tasks. Those being introduced like to feel that the person reaching out to them is simply a warm and caring person - and that will almost always be the case. What people start doing as a volunteer "job" often becomes a pleasure with the passage of time.

Building Quality

"Listen, I don't like coming off as this superior, judgmental person, but you're the one who asked for it. Why didn't we come back to the church again? I suppose we were spoiled by the church we belonged to in Columbus, but I guess our standards are just different than what people expect in your church. The choir was mediocre, the sermon was mediocre, the whole service was mediocre. The Sunday school class we attended was worse than mediocre; it was bad. People spent the first twenty minutes talking about how to handle transportation to this ball game everyone in the group wanted to attend. It was like they had to reach this big consensus on meeting at the church to travel together or on just meeting at the game. Why couldn't the people in charge have made a decision? Sitting through too many discussions like that would make me crazy. Then I found out why people didn't mind spending so much time talking about travel plans, because the teacher was unprepared and didn't know how to handle the class. We were going around the circle reading the lesson aloud like a class of third graders."

"The youth group at the church didn't hold my daughter's interest. The advisor tried to draw her into the discussion, but it was very clear that the other kids didn't care what she had to say. The meeting was supposed to start at six o'clock. I brought her to the church a few minutes before six, and it turned out to be almost six-thirty before even the advisor showed up. It was almost seven before any organized activities started. That's not exactly a comfortable situation for a visitor to the group. Things were supposed to end at eight-thirty. I waited in the parking lot until nine, when she finally came out to go home. She said the other kids were still going strong and might be there until nine-thirty or ten. She didn't want to stay."

"The people at the church seemed to be nice. I think people

were glad to have us visit, and there are some ways in which we could be happy there. I don't regret the month that we spent attending services and special events, but there were just too many things that didn't feel quite right. The nursery wasn't quite as nice as I'd like to see. The bulletin and the newsletter always have typos and don't feel professionally done. Your minister seems to know a lot about the Bible, but I didn't get anything from his sermons that I could apply to my daily life. My wife is going through a difficult time at work, and she needs to feel nourished. That didn't happen in your church. The quality of almost everything was a little lacking."

The three speakers just quoted are each talking about a different local church. They were part of a group interviewed in an effort to understand why people visited a particular congregation but then decided not to actually join the church. All of those who were interviewed had to be prompted to share what they honestly felt. They didn't feel comfortable being critical of a church, but those were honest feelings and also fairly accurate observations.

The first chapter of this book discusses the reality that simply having quality programming in the church isn't sufficient to have church growth. That reality is certainly true. It's also true, however, that failure to meet reasonably high standards of quality will keep people who visit from joining a church.

Manufacturing companies in the United States have been placing increasingly great emphasis on an approach to quality which was first developed by Dr. W. Edwards Deming. When Deming first began to articulate his ideas on the importance of quality and on how to obtain it, he did not find an especially receptive audience in the United States. His 1950 lectures to Japanese business leaders, however, brought an enthusiastic response. Manufacturing companies in Japan were among the first to embrace Deming's philosophy, which has only in recent years begun to have comparable impact in the United States.

In his book *Quest for Quality in the Church*, Ezra Earl Jones offers this definition of quality: "Quality is getting more than you expect. Quality is providing a service or product that is consistently superior. . . . Quality goes beyond expectations to delight and surprise people" [p.7]. If quality is sufficiently emphasized in a church, visitors should leave feeling not just satisfied but deeply pleased, even surprised.

Long-time members of a church are not as likely to be unhappy about low quality programs as are those who visit the church. Those who have been part of the congregation for many years have formed strong friendships within the church and are often willing to overlook lapses in the quality of what is offered. While some people are very critical of the pastor, the typical active member of a congregation builds a bond with the pastor over a period of time. As a result of that bond, people tend to be kind in their assessments of how the minister performs.

During the summer of 1993, a group of churches in the Midwest invited visitors and members to "grade" the church in several areas. The following scale was used:

    5 = A   (excellent)
    4 = B   (good)
    3 = C   (fair)
    2 = D   (poor)
    1 = F   (failing)

The difference in perspective between visitors and members was significant, with members having in each category a more positive view of what the church offered than visitors:

What Grade Would You Give?	Visitors	Members	Difference
Parking	3.9	4.5	0.6
Greeters	4.4	4.6	0.2
Sermon	3.4	4.3	0.9
Music	4.1	4.4	0.3
Nursery	4.1	4.7	0.6
Restrooms	4.2	4.3	0.1
Sunday School	3.9	4.1	0.2
Warmth	3.8	4.7	0.9

The grades are shown on the next page in chart form.

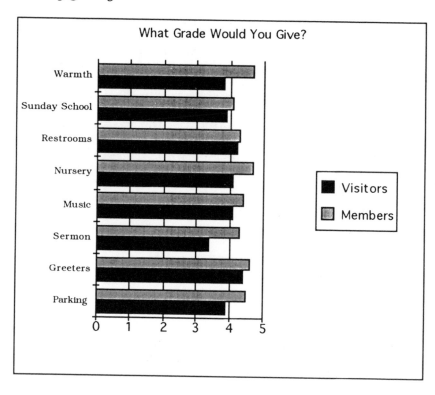

What Grade Would You Give?

The differences are especially pronounced in the evaluation of the sermon and in the assessment of congregational warmth. Visitors, who in most instances did not know the pastor at all before attending, were far more critical of the sermon than were members of the congregation. In reflecting on that difference, it's important to note that the average age of the visitors was younger than that of church members. Younger people, on the whole, have more difficulty accepting the sermon as a medium and are thus especially inclined to be critical in that area. Their evaluation of the music at the worship services, however, was almost as positive as that of members.

Most churches like to see themselves as warm and accepting. That is not, however, always the image which comes across to those who visit. The pronounced difference in that area suggests that much work needs to be done on how members respond to visitors.

There were also rather large differences between how visitors and members viewed the parking convenience and the condition of the nursery. Members already know where to park and have a tendency to take parking for granted. Visitors are concerned about parking and may not be comfortable crossing a street if they have young children.

Because of the younger average age of the visitors, they were more likely to utilize the nursery facilities than were the members. Thus the condition of the nursery was a theoretical question for many of the members but a very pragmatic question for those visitors who had small children to leave in the nursery.

A total of seventy-three churches took part in the study. It's especially interesting to examine the five churches which received the highest average grades from visitors and members alike. The discrepancies between the perceptions of visitors and members are not so great in those congregations, and the average scores are higher in almost every category. The following chart provides scores from those five churches:

What Grade Would You Give?	Visitors	Members	Difference
Parking	4.6	4.7	0.1
Greeters	4.7	4.7	0
Sermon	4.4	4.6	0.2
Music	4.5	4.6	0.1
Nursery	4.8	4.8	0
Restrooms	4.6	4.7	0.1
Sunday School	4.4	4.5	0.1
Warmth	4.5	4.8	0.3

The largest discrepancy between the evaluation of visitors and the evaluation of members remained in the areas of perceived congregational warmth and of the sermon. The gaps, however, are much smaller: .3 for congregational warmth and .2 for the sermon. The smaller discrepancies between the evaluations of visitors and of members makes it appear that the members in those churches hold somewhat higher standards than do the members in some of the other churches in the study.

It's also interesting to compare what was actually happening in terms of growth and decline in those five churches with the others which participated in the study. Three of the five churches which excelled by the evaluation of both visitors and members were in fact growing. Two of those three churches had been emphasizing church growth for several years, had many members who invited friends and neighbors to church, and had careful follow-up plans in place for those who attended. The third growing church did not have as systematic plans in place for church growth as the other two but was located in a rapidly growing suburb; the church did do careful follow-up on all who attended.

The other two churches, in spite of the high evaluations of the quality of their worship services, facilities, and programs, were both experiencing some decline. One of them, a large downtown church, had begun more aggressive advertising and had initiated a careful plan to follow up on visitors starting in 1990. As a result, though not yet growing, the church had significantly slowed the rate of decline. During the nineteen-eighties, that church had lost an average of more than seventy members a year. For the first three years of the nineties, the average yearly loss had dropped to twenty-one.

The other church, a medium-sized congregation in an older, fairly stable part of the same community as the downtown church, has been involved in a number of important community ministries but has done very little about intentional church growth. Their community involvement helps generate a flow of visitors, but they have had no systematic plans for follow-up. They have experienced an average loss of seven members a year for the past decade.

Those five churches show some interesting connections among these factors:

- High quality programming
- Intentional church growth strategies
- Demographic influence

All three of those factors affect what happens in church growth and decline. The two churches with high quality programming, intentional church growth strategies, and reasonable demographic characteristics are showing healthy growth. The third growing church is not quite as intentional about growth strategies, but has good visitor follow-up and the benefits of an excellent demographic situation with the area around it growing rapidly.

The downtown church offers high quality programming and shows considerable innovation in church growth strategies. Yet the problems of the downtown area are significant enough that all their efforts have only slowed the rate of decline rather than actually moving the church into a growth mode. It will be interesting to see what happens over the next few years.

While the church with the strong community emphasis is not losing members rapidly, it is nevertheless not growing in spite of the fact that it is a reasonably stable area in terms of demographics and offers high quality programming. I am convinced that a few changes in intentionality of outreach and follow-up could turn that into a growing congregation.

It's also interesting to note that of the bottom forty churches in terms of quality ranking by visitors and members, all but four are declining in membership. Those four are simply holding even. None of those churches is growing, and it does not appear likely that they will do so. A few of those churches have become more serious about intentional efforts at church growth, but the low quality of their programming stands as a barrier to turning visitors into prospective members and prospective members into fully assimilated members.

A church which wants to grow must be intentional in growth strategies and intentional in the development of high quality programming. Secular organizations are increasingly seeing issues of quality as central to the marketing process. While the church certainly differs in significant ways from secular organizations, there is much that we can learn in this area. The following pages offer a marketing look at your church which incorporates both issues of quality and of intentionality in growth strategies. Feel free to reproduce these pages for use in your local church. You may also wish to examine the more open-ended marketing questionnaire which appears in my book *Plain Talk About Church Growth*.

A Marketing Look At Your Church

"Grade" your church on each of the items which follows according to this scale:

 5 = A   (excellent)
 4 = B   (good)
 3 = C   (fair)
 2 = D   (poor)
 1 = F   (failing)

If an item does not apply to your church, leave it blank. You may want to consider whether or not items left blank represent programs which should be initiated.

Getting People to Our Church

_____ The quality of the training we have provided to help members feel comfortable inviting people to church.

_____ The quality of the training we have provided to help members feel comfortable sharing their faith with others.

_____ The quality of our outreach, through canvasses or in other ways, to the neighborhood around the church and to any other neighborhoods in which we have a concentration of members.

_____ The quality of printed information we have about our church to be shared with prospective members.

_____ The quality of the signs which point the way to our church.

_____ The quality of the sign(s) on our church property.

_____ The quality of our yellow pages advertisement.

_____ The quality of our news releases.

_____ The quality of any paid advertising we do through newspapers, radio, or television.

When People Arrive At the Church

_____ The quality of our parking arrangements.

_____ The exterior appearance of our building.

_____ The warmth and helpfulness of our greeters.

_____ The attractiveness of our hallways and restrooms.

_____ The quality of our printed information for visitors.

_____ The quality of our bulletin boards.

_____ The quality of our nursery facilities, including the staff.

_____ The quality of the coffee/fellowship time provided.

_____ The quality of our facilities for the physically handicapped.

Worship Services

_____ The quality of our ushering.

_____ The appearance and helpfulness of the bulletin.

_____ The way we make announcements and share concerns (from the perspective of a visitor).

_____ Our music program.

_____ The quality of the sermons (or drama or other medium if you have a contemporary service).

_____ The clarity of our instructions on baptism and communion.

_____ The quality and ease of our registration system.

_____ The warmth with which members respond to visitors.

Sunday School or Other Christian Education Offerings

_____ The quality of our children's classes.

_____ The attractiveness of our children's classrooms.

_____ The quality of our youth classes.

_____ The attractiveness of our youth meeting area.

_____ The quality of our adult classes.

_____ The attractiveness of our adult classrooms.

_____ The manner in which visitors are made to feel welcome in classes.

_____ The clarity of instructions on what children should do when Sunday school ends (wait for their parents, go to the fellowship area, etc.).

The Quality of Our Follow-Up on Visitors

_____ The promptness with which visitors receive a visit at their home.

_____ The quality of the initial visits that are made to visitors.

_____ The system that we have in place for continued contact with visitors who keep coming, through faith friends, mentors, or another strategy.

_____ The clearing house we've established to share information about visitors to worship, Sunday school classes, and other groups in the church.

_____ The quality of the training received by people who do volunteer visiting in homes.

Youth Group

_____ The quality of our youth group programming.

_____ The way visitors to the youth group are welcomed.

_____ The training our young people have received on how to reach out to their friends.

The Church Office and Related Matters

_____ The quality of greeting and information shared by our church secretary or volunteers in the office with visitors to the office and any others who make inquiries.

_____ The quality of our newsletter.

_____ The quality of any communications sent out by our church.

Programming for Various Groups

_____ The quality of our nursery school and/or day care programs.

_____ The quality of our Vacation Bible School.

In responding to the next few items, assess the quality and adequacy of your total programming for each group, including Sunday school activities.

_____ The quality of our total programming for children.

_____ The quality of our total programming for youth.

_____ The quality of our total programming for women.

_____ The quality of our total programming for men.

_____ The quality of our total programming for young adult singles (18-35 years of age).

_____ The quality of our total programming for young adult couples (18-35 years of age).

_____ The quality of our total programming for parents of children.

_____ The quality of our total programming for parents of teenagers.

_____ The quality of our total programming for middle-aged people.

_____ The quality of our total programming for senior citizens.

Assimilating Members

_____ The quality of our membership preparation process.

_____ The quickness of our response when people break a pattern of regular attendance.

_____ The quality of our efforts to help newer and older members become well acquainted.

_____ The quality of our work in promptly involving new members in ministry and service through the church.

Ministerial Style:
Asset or Liability?

"I should be doing more about church growth, but I can't seem to find the time. This church has very high expectations of the pastor. When a member is having surgery, the assumption is that I'll be present to say a prayer before the operation, sit with the family in the hospital waiting room during the surgery, and then be there when the person wakes up after the anesthetic wears off. This isn't a big church, but it doesn't take many hospital admissions to throw your whole week off schedule. . . . I can see that kind of thing when a person is having open heart surgery or brain surgery, but it doesn't seem necessary for the removal of an appendix or a gall bladder. . . . I know ministers in other denominations who give good pastoral care without devoting quite as much time. They might come around the night before the surgery to visit and say a prayer and then come by late in the day of the surgery to see how things went. They wouldn't spend between six and eight hours that day just involved with one family unless it was a very major surgery. With the size of their churches, they can't."

"Some people accuse me of being dictatorial. They may be right, but I like to think of myself as a benevolent dictator. In this church, people expect the pastor to set the pace and the priorities for everything that happens. That's part of the job. I can get good support for almost anything that I say is important. Of course that also means my neck is on the line when something doesn't work out. If I were wrong too many times, I'd probably stop receiving so much strong support. . . . Sometimes, unfortunately, people start to think of this as being *my* church. That isn't healthy, and I'm not comfortable with it. I'll leave here someday, and I wonder what will happen to all these members who joined especially because of their attraction to my sermons and my style of ministry."

"This church could probably be growing faster if I helped people be more intentional. The problem is that things almost seem out of control right now. We're trying to do so many different things, and it seems to me that the paid staff and the volunteers are stretched about as thinly as they can be. There's also a limit to how much change people can accept in a given period of time. Instead of theology and Bible study, I needed more seminary training in time management and organizational structure."

The three clergy just quoted are pastoring very different congregations and have developed styles of ministry which are just as different. The first speaker feels the weight of high congregational expectations, especially in the area of pastoral care. The church he's pastoring has been in decline for several years, and he's painfully aware that he hasn't done enough toward reversing that decline. He doesn't know how to free up the time and energy for change.

The second speaker described himself as a "benevolent dictator." He has *the* major leadership role in the church and has considerable freedom to set priorities for the church's program. Many people have been attracted to the church because of his high community visibility (and rather charismatic personality). He has legitimate concern about what those people who have joined primarily because of his presence will do when he is no longer pastor there.

The third minister is serving a medium-sized church in a rapidly growing area. Although the church has not been as intentional about growth as it perhaps should be, considerable growth has nevertheless been taking place. The minister who is quoted is committed to preparing high quality sermons and to giving high quality pastoral care (though not at the expense in time that the first speaker experienced). While she loves the ministry and the people of the church, she feels that the pace of change and the demands on leadership are somewhat out of control.

Many different factors work together to determine the style of ministry which one practices:

- The individual minister's personality

- The style of ministry observed by the minister while growing up.

- The seminary training received by the minister.

- The theological and biblical view of ministry which is developed over the years.

- The expectations of clergy which are present in the denomination and which are expressed by denominational executives.

- The expectations of the local church where the pastor works.

- The expectations of the spouse, children, and parents of the minister.

- The relationship with Christ and the developing spiritual life of the minister.

For me to presume in the space of one chapter of one book to recommend the single best ministerial style would be unrealistic and also unhelpful. There are limits to how much change in style any of us as clergy are capable of making and also limits on how much change in style the churches we serve are capable of accepting.

There is no question, however, but that from the standpoint of church growth, some aspects of ministerial style are more important and more helpful than others. My consulting work in the area of church growth and the responses I've received from clergy and laity to numerous surveys leave me with the clear conviction that the pastor does play the single most important role of any individual in determining whether or not a church grows to its potential. With that reality in mind, I offer the following perspectives on ministerial style. Please keep in mind that I am speaking from the perspective of an advocate of church growth. I readily recognize that there are additional priorities which every pastor must evaluate and that some of the suggestions I offer will simply not be compatible with the style or philosophy of some ministers.

1. The minister needs to set the example in the quest for quality in the church's overall program and ministry. The level of quality of program, ministry, and outreach to which the minister is committed is a limiting factor for the church. In *Quest for Quality in the Church*, Ezra Earl Jones writes that true quality "begins with the leader. You can get only the amount of quality in an organization that the leader is capable of and disposed to leading" [p.43].

As discussed in the previous chapter, people have increasingly high expectations of the church in terms of quality. No congregation is going to reach its potential without a major emphasis on improving its program, ministry, and outreach. The minister is in a unique position to urge high quality throughout the church by:

- Modeling quality in his or her own work, especially in worship leadership, sermons, and pastoral care.

- Teaching boards, committees, task forces, and classes better ways to accomplish their tasks.

- Helping create a vision of quality so high that it not only meets the expectations of members and visitors but exceeds those expectations.

- Urging careful, objective evaluation of the quality of ministry in the church as perceived by both members and visitors. Using "report cards" in the bulletin and asking members and visitors to "grade" various aspects of the life of the church can be one approach to this process. This isn't something to do every single Sunday, but it is a good exercise over one or two months of time every year.

- Seeking regular feedback about his or her own performance and expressing appreciation to those who offer positive suggestions for change.

- Helping improve and emphasizing the church's Christian education program, which is a vitally important component of the church's ministry and outreach which often doesn't receive enough recognition. The book *Reaching Out Through Christian Education* offers many practical strategies in this area of concern.

2. The minister needs to cultivate an intimate relationship with God and pay more attention to God's guidance than to expectations of the denomination or the local church. James Fowler writes in *Weaving the New Creation* of the danger that comes when clergy are not open to the Spirit: "[M]any clergy in my denomination and others have developed a franchise mentality that, like tenure in the university, can make security, modest institutional gains, and lock-step career advancement the main goal of ministry, while avoiding the risks, conflict, and spiritual challenge that keep us open to the deep movements and guidance of the Spirit" [p.150].

When the minister fails to cultivate a close relationship with God, then he or she can all too easily become a victim of multiple demands and influences from many different persons. While the expectations and needs of most of those persons should be heard, the primary loyalty of the minister must always be to Christ.

Many clergy get caught in the trap of struggling to accommodate the expectations of everyone with whom they work. The list can include family members, church members, denominational officials, and a wide range of people in the community. The combined desires or expectations of so many different people are far more than any individual can meet. Some of those desires or expectations will even be contradictory! Many ministers frequently find themselves faced with several different and important events at the same time. One minister recently shared with me that on a single evening, various people were hoping that he would:

- Attend a parent-teacher meeting at his daughter's school.

- Attend an important board meeting at the church.

- Be present at the funeral home with a family who had just suffered a loss through an automobile accident.

- Share in a meeting of local clergy on ways to work cooperatively to lower incidents of violence in the community.

All four were important events, and the minister wanted to be present at each one. There was no way, however, that he could do that. He was also aware that two new families had visited the church on Sunday and that he had not yet found time in the week to call on them; other priorities had continued to make it impossible for him to do so.

There are many time management and priority setting plans which can be of help to clergy. The foundation of decision-making in these areas, however, needs to be based on the minister's own relationship with Christ rather than on the expectations of any other individual or group. The minister who focuses first on living as Christ wishes will find the other decisions easier ones to make.

3. The minister needs to take control of his or her own priority setting and time management. Ministers too often are caught simply reacting to the needs and concerns which arise on a daily and weekly basis. Functioning in this way ends up becoming a form of crisis management which makes it difficult or impossible for the minister to influence the overall direction of the church as an organization.

The second suggestion made speaks to this aspect of style by emphasizing the necessity of cultivating a close relationship with God. That relationship then becomes the single most important factor in decision-making. The minister, however, must still choose to take control of priority setting and time management. There are plenty of other people ready and willing to set the priorities and claim the time of the pastor!

My consulting experiences and the sharing clergy and laity have done with me on surveys make me painfully aware that there are churches in which clergy are viewed as "hired help." Churches with that attitude generally have a strong core of laity who exercise the major control over the life of the church.

Instead of the problem being a minister who exercises too much control, the problem becomes a small group of laity who exercise too much control. That small group generally consists of people who are very happy with the church as it is and are not very interested in seeing growth and the accompanying change.

The "hired help" view of the pastorate is common in denominations which have a relatively "low" view of the professional ministry. By contrast, an example of a "high" view would be that of the Roman Catholic Church in which the pope, cardinals, bishops, and priests are viewed not only as "set-apart" for their ministry but also as occupying such a special relationship with Christ that they are not permitted to marry.

Historically, a lower view of the role and importance of a set-apart ministry has been connected with a higher view of the importance of the ministry of all Christians. Within that tradition, the set-apart or "employed" minister differs from others in having received a seminary education with a solid theological background, biblical knowledge, pastoral care skills, and at least some understanding of the church as an organization. That perspective should, in theory, lead to a ministry which is truly shared by all those in the church, with the set-apart minister bringing theological background and other specific knowledge and skills to that shared work.

Unfortunately, the common result of the lower view of the professional ministry is not the elevation of the importance of the work done by every member of the church but a lowering of respect for the set-apart minister. The minister begins to be viewed in the same way that an employee who worked a forty hour week in the private sector would be viewed. The employee in the private sector, however, would normally only have one supervisor rather than a church full of them and would be paid overtime for working more than forty hours a week!

The minister is normally the person in the church who is best able to look at the overall concerns which exist in the congregation and to help people develop a realistic view of what needs to be accomplished for the building up of the church as the body of Christ and to further the ministry of the church to the world. It's impossible for a minister to accomplish this if he or she is not in control of personal priorities and time management.

Clergy in denominations which have a much "higher" view of the ordained ministry can, of course, also become caught in the trap of losing control over personal priorities and time management. Part of what motivates many people to enter the ministry is a desire to meet the needs of people and to merit their appreciation and approval. Attempting to meet the needs and expectations of too many different people can create a workload which is overwhelming, even if one works the eighty and ninety hour weeks which are commonplace for some clergy.

In terms of church growth concerns, it's not realistic to expect members of the congregation to recognize the importance of outreach and to make it a priority on their volunteer time if the minister fails to set the example. That doesn't mean neglecting the pastoral needs of the congregation or ignoring other needs of the congregation. As previously discussed in this book, the quality of the church's overall program and ministry is important in its own right and also has very direct impact on church growth. While high quality permeating the life of the church will not automatically result in growth, the absence of quality will make growth difficult or impossible. If the church is going to grow, however, the minister must give outreach related concerns some priority on time and energy. Practical consequences of that might include:

- Placing scheduling priority on meetings with a church growth committee or task force.

- Teaching faith sharing skills to boards and committees of the church.

- Preaching a series of sermons about the need to share our faith with others.

- Setting aside one afternoon and one evening a week for the purpose of making follow-up calls on prospective members.

- Including reading and study on church growth strategies as part of personal study time.

4. The minister has an important teaching function to perform in helping church leaders understand what has happened in terms of church growth or decline in the past

and in helping them understand the actions necessary for growth to occur. While church officers and other leaders can help gather statistical information about the history of growth and decline in the congregation, the minister is usually the person best qualified to help members understand that history. The minister will normally also be the person who has had the greatest exposure to strategies for church growth and who has the most current information on effective outreach.

If the minister does not feel personally qualified to perform this teaching function, then he or she needs to recruit and assist qualified lay persons in this task. If a church has had a lengthy history of decline in membership, it is absolutely crucial for key leadership to become aware of some of the reasons for that decline and to identify strategies to reverse the decline. For the minister to avoid dealing with this reality would be like a restaurant manager doing nothing new with publicity, menu, or pricing in spite of fewer meals being served every year. Continuing to ignore the problem means that the restaurant will eventually be closed and the restaurant manager out of a job.

Many churches have not been sufficiently concerned about witnessing to the unchurched, church growth, or member assimilation to develop a comprehensive plan for outreach. As people become aware of the realities of growth or decline in their congregation, they should become increasingly open to a plan which includes strategies for:

- Teaching members how to comfortably invite friends, neighbors, and coworkers to church.

- Teaching members how to comfortably share their faith with others.

- Utilizing brochures, mailings, the yellow pages, and news media in effective ways.

- Improving the appearance and image of the church.

- Training greeters, ushers, teachers, and other leaders in how to effectively welcome visitors.

- Having a comprehensive plan for follow-up

on those who visit the church.

- Offering an effective membership orientation process.

- Modifying the structure of the church as needed so that new members can be actively involved in the church's ministry.

- Becoming intentional about bringing together older and newer members of the congregation in positive ways.

5. Ministers should help church members become more comfortable talking about their faith and reaching out to nonmembers. Many people are truly not comfortable talking about their faith in Christ. Their faith may be deep, but they find it awkward to express it verbally. While some persons feel their faith is so personal that they don't want to talk about it, most would like to feel more comfortable discussing faith issues.

Clergy, trained by education and experience to talk about matters of faith, can provide important help to church members in this area. Some of the ways clergy and other trained staff can help in this process include:

- Acting as resource persons and helping train volunteer visitors, faith friends, and member sponsors.

- Forming study groups using a resource like this book or *Plain Talk About Church Growth*.

- Encouraging all kinds of Bible study and spiritual life groups in the parish. While these groups aren't focused on member recruitment, the experiences in these groups help people feel more comfortable talking about their faith.

- Helping Sunday school classes and other Christian education groups better understand the role they can play in church growth. *Reaching Out Through Christian Education* offers several suggestions for helping people become more comfortable talking about their faith and inviting others to church.

- Using the pulpit to encourage people to share their faith and providing practical suggestions to help in that process.

- Making it clear that they are available as resource persons about spiritual matters and always willing to talk with people about faith issues. This should seem an obvious item, but people sometimes are reluctant to seek such help out of fear of appearing foolish. Ministers can let people know through the pulpit and church groups that there are no foolish questions where matters of faith are concerned.

6. Ministers should set high standards for the way that visitors to the church are welcomed. Most people who come to a church's worship services or Sunday school classes as visitors want to feel genuinely, warmly welcomed - but they don't want to be put on the spot or embarrassed. Many churches have a tendency to fall into one of two extremes in their welcome to visitors:

- **Extreme One:** Putting visitors on the spot by introducing them to the whole congregation during the worship service and by attempting to personally introduce them to everyone who is available during the fellowship time. Those who fall into this extreme will often ask very pointedly if the visitors want to join the church. Unless the visitors themselves express an immediate interest in joining, that question is better shared during a conversation in the home of the visitor - after more information about the church has been shared.

- **Extreme Two:** Almost completely ignoring the presence of visitors and letting them stand alone during the fellowship time. This extreme doesn't risk putting visitors on the spot - it risks making visitors think no one cares that they've come. Some churches function in this way because many members are not comfortable introducing themselves to other people and fear rejection.

The minister needs to create a climate which helps visitors

111

feel warmly received without putting them on the spot or embarrassing them. Some components of that climate include:

- Having greeters and ushers trained to greet people with warmth but not to be pushy. The minister should also be sure that greeters and ushers have the information available to answer common inquiries of visitors and prospective members.

- Using a registration process during the worship service which gets the church needed information about visitors without putting the visitors on the spot with the whole congregation. Many churches effectively utilize registration pads which are passed from one end of the pew to the other and then back again. Those who are members and those who are nonmembers alike complete lines on the registration pads (including address and phone), and there are spaces to check to indicate member or visitor status. By passing the pads back the opposite direction in the pews, every person has opportunity to read the names of others in the pew. This procedure makes it easier for church members in the same pew to reach out to visitors.

- Offering an informal time during the worship service when people greet those seated around them, and having a fellowship time available when members can mix with visitors before or after the worship service(s).

- Taking the initiative to introduce himself or herself to visitors and also introducing the visitors to a few other people after the service or during a fellowship time.

7. While ministers should not do all the visiting and other outreach to prospective members, they should model a willingness to visit in homes, offer support to volunteers who are doing so, and ensure that valuable information about prospective members is not lost. Even if a minister's schedule makes it possible to personally call on the home of each person, couple, or family who visit the church, that staff outreach is not a substitute for contact being made by a member of the congregation. When a minister calls at the home of a visitor, it's possible for that to be interpreted as fulfilling a vocational responsibility. When a lay person calls at the home of a visitor, it's immediately clear that the lay person is showing a very personal, open interest.

Volunteers are not, however, going to be enthusiastic about calling in homes unless it's clear that the minister is also doing so. Many of the most rapidly growing congregations respond to the first visit of an individual, couple, or family by having two calls made at the home within the first week. The first call is made within forty-eight hours by a lay volunteer (or couple) and often includes bringing baked goods and literature about the church. Then the minister or another staff member makes a call later in the week to answer any questions and to extend an invitation to services on Sunday. Even if demands on the minister's time do not permit a call on every first time visitor, those persons who indicate strong interest in the church by repeated visits need to be called on by the pastor.

The minister needs to seek every possible opportunity to express appreciation and reinforcement to lay volunteers who are following up on first time visitors and who are working as faith friends or mentors to prospective members and new members. The volunteer outreach is extremely important to the church, and the pastor's reinforcement of those efforts is always appreciated.

The pastor can also help give perspective when volunteers become discouraged because those they have visited do not immediately decide to join the church. Not every person who visits will join the congregation, and some people require a few months of contact with the church before they are willing to make the decision to become members. Volunteers need help keeping these realities in perspective so that they don't lose enthusiasm, become too pushy, or simply stop making the contacts.

The minister also needs to see that careful records are maintained on the attendance of prospective members and on the contacts which are made with these persons by staff and volunteers. Those records can be maintained in the church office or by a volunteer, but it is important that they be kept current and that information be shared with appropriate persons such as Sunday school teachers, youth advisors, and choir directors who can help involve prospective members in the life of the church.

8. The minister needs to see his or her work in church growth as part of a team effort. The second quotation at the start of this chapter spoke of the difficulty which comes when people join the church primarily because of the style and the personality of the pastor. Because of the minister's high visibility in the church and often in the community as well, that situation can't entirely be avoided. Certainly the church wants to welcome those persons who join because of the pastor, but it's also important for the final commitment of those persons to be to Christ rather than to any individual. The minister can help with this potential problem by intentionally making church growth a team process. Some clergy and laity like the athletic analogy in which the pastor is the coach. Seeing church growth as a team effort means, among other things:

- Working cooperatively with lay persons who are actively following up on visitors - so that there is mutual support and sharing of needed information.

- Helping the entire congregation come to see sharing the faith and helping the church grow as part of the responsibility of each person. Most growing churches have high percentages of the congregation extending invitations to friends, neighbors, and coworkers. Growing churches also have almost everyone involved in helping visitors and new members feel welcome and accepted.

- Seeing that new members are truly assimilated into the congregation and helping them to form a variety of relationships and become involved in a ministry of the church.

Other Barriers to Growth

Church Conflict

All churches have diversity in membership, and some of the healthiest churches have the greatest diversity. Differences of opinion go along with diversity and can create a stimulating atmosphere which will be attractive to some people who are searching for a church home.

Outright conflict is another matter. While there are some people who thrive on battle, most are already dealing with enough potential conflict situations in their homes and at work. They aren't particularly interested in a church which is in the midst of a major conflict. By "major conflict," I mean a situation in which one of the following is happening:

- The congregation is in danger of having a split between two large groups of members, whatever the reason for the potential split may be.

- The congregation is strongly divided over the leadership of the pastor to such an extent that the departure of the pastor or of a large number of members appears likely to happen soon.

- Enough members of the congregation are upset that worship attendance and financial support have declined by 20% or more within a single year.

In any of those situations, it may be necessary for the church to work through the conflict before initiating a strong church growth effort. Failure to do so may result in efforts at outreach being relatively ineffective and on any new members who are recruited finding themselves very uncomfortable in the church.

Most churches which are experiencing conflict strong enough to be characterized by the results I've described need to be seeking the help of a consultant from outside the congregation to assist them in working through the situation. There are denominational agencies and private consultants who specialize in helping churches deal with that kind of conflict.

Congregations going through periods of difference of opinion with less serious consequences should move ahead with church growth initiatives. Differences of opinion are inevitable, and the church that waits until there is no minor conflict taking place will probably never grow. It's also inevitable that a few members will occasionally leave a church, feeling that they will be happier elsewhere. A church can be very healthy and still lose a few members by transfer to other congregations in the same community and may also receive a few members by transfer from other congregations in the same community.

The changes which accompany a church growth initiative can occasionally result in the loss of a few members, though good pastoral care can help minimize that. It's only deep conflict affecting the entire congregation that is sufficient reason not to move forward with efforts at church growth. No matter what the level of conflict, the church should still respond warmly to those persons who choose to visit.

Organizational Structures That Impede Growth

In medium and large membership churches, many people tend to ignore the organizational structure. The leadership in those congregations and much of the membership in smaller churches, however, will initially feel uncomfortable with changes in the official structure, in the way that persons are selected for boards and committees, and in the way that decisions are made. No one wants to lightly undertake changes in these areas of the life of the church, but there are situations in which the structure of the church has become a significant liability to recruiting and assimilating new members:

1. Some churches have extremely cumbersome structures for decision-making. This can be especially true for churches which use full congregational meetings for many different decisions. The emphasis on participatory democracy in these congregations has many positive aspects, but it can make innovation very difficult and can consume vast amounts of time making decisions which sometimes affect very few people. Prospective members who are unchurched will generally not be patient with a ponderous decision-making process.

If your church has a slow, awkward structure for decision-making, you may wish to consider streamlining that process by giving more authority to task forces and committees rather than requiring that so many decisions pass through multiple groups or even end up being considered by the congregation as a whole. This requires a slightly greater level of trust, but will often free up many hours of volunteer time for outreach. Church of the Savior in Washington, D.C. makes interesting use of "mission groups" which are formed by members who share a common concern and which have broad authority to go ahead and act unless a decision will truly impact the entire church.

2. If it is impossible to add members to any board, commission, or committee except at the time of an annual election, then that process should be reviewed. Experience in congregations all across the country continues to confirm that new members need to quickly be involved in the life of the church. Making someone who joins the church wait for many months before being able to share in the work of a church group can create real problems in assimilating that person. Growing churches generally have a more open view which permits additional persons to be added to church organizations at any time during the year. If your structure is such that making this kind of change is next to impossible as far as formal membership on boards, commissions, or committees is concerned, then consider some kind of honorary status, perhaps without vote, on these groups.

At the same time as one works to open the structure of boards and other groups, it's also important to remember that committee membership is not the only way to involve people in the church. A great many people, especially those in the young adult years, would rather be part of a group which is involved in direct action and ministry than be part of a committee which has many meetings but does little in terms of direct action. The mission groups described previously are generally open to anyone who wants to share in the goals and work of the group.

Short-Term Focus

Congregations which undertake church growth initiatives often expect too much in a short period of time. If your church membership has been in decline for many years, it isn't realistic to expect that a single year of church growth efforts will reverse that decline. Church leaders must often learn new strategies for reaching out to others, and the whole congregation must become part of a more open stance toward visitors and prospective members. These changes take time.

While there are many ways to publicize new efforts of your church, the best publicity is often word of mouth, and that is sometimes a slow process. New social groups for young adults, support groups for persons experiencing difficult life situations, and alternative worship services should all be started with as strong a core of people as possible; but you shouldn't despair when those groups don't immediately begin growing. Keep working to improve publicity and to involve existing church members in telling their friends, neighbors, and coworkers about the new activities in your church.

As shared in an earlier chapter: ***Most people greatly over-estimate the amount of change which can be accomplished in one year and greatly underestimate the amount which can be accomplished in five to ten years.*** That's true for individuals, businesses, communities, and churches.

Fear of Change

In many different ways, I've talked in this book about strategies to help churches make needed changes. The process of change, of course, can be threatening to a congregation. The addition of new members can be frightening to older members who fear they will no longer have as much control and may not have their own needs met.

If fear of change constitutes one of the major barriers for your church in terms of growth, consider these specific strategies:

1. Create an ad hoc, long-range planning committee to study what has happened to your church in the past and to make plans for the future. An ad hoc committee will generally be more open to the possibility of change than one of the standing committees of the church would be. Most organizations, including the church, aren't likely to become enthusiastic about change unless leaders and members first become dissatisfied with the status quo.

A long-range planning committee which looks carefully at the past and present of the church before making recommendations for the future can help create a better climate for change. Think carefully about the best persons to have on that group both in terms of openness to change and in terms of congregational support for the results of the planning efforts. Lyle Schaller's book *Create Your Own Future!* gives excellent counsel for the work of such a group.

2. Work to provide high quality pastoral care to the existing membership while in the midst of a church growth initiative. If members feel that the pastor and other church leaders are still concerned about them, they will find it easier to be supportive of growth efforts. For the pastor, this may mean spending less time with boards and committees and more time in direct ministry to individuals. Such care can often be improved through a neighborhood shepherding program or a church caregiver program.

3. Remember the value of trying new ideas on a trial or experimental basis. It's usually easier to win approval for that kind of innovation, and this gives opportunity for people to become comfortable with the change before making it permanent.

4. You sometimes can get people to withhold their disapproval even if they are not fully willing to endorse a new idea. That can give you permission to move ahead cautiously and show people in time that the change brings good results.

5. Remember that there are limits on how much change members can accept in a given period of time. It's possible for even the most progressive congregation to be overdosed on change. Determine which changes are the most important in order to meet the goals of the church, and then initiate those in a logical way - not necessarily all at the same time!

6. Also keep in mind the reality that congregations must sometimes say NO to a change once or even twice before saying YES. This can be especially true with building programs and with relocations.

For more help in the area of change, refer to Lyle Schaller's *Strategies for Change* or to Paul Mundey's *Change and the Established Congregation.*

Financial Barriers

While many of the strategies suggested in this book require volunteer time more than significant funds, there can be occasions when a limited supply of money makes it difficult for a congregation to do needed advertising, add necessary staff, or make needed improvements to physical facilities related to church growth. Some congregations have successfully implemented a strategy of packaging the various things needed for improvement of quality and for numerical growth into a special financial program that is outside the regular budget of the church, much like a building program might be. Members are then asked to make pledges above their regular level of giving for a specific period of time, most commonly three to five years. That provides opportunity for new initiatives and gives a period of time in which the strength of the membership and of regular financial giving can be improved.

Things You Can Do For Growth - Even If No One Wants To Cooperate !

While reading this book, you may have identified several ideas and strategies which can be used for growth in your church. You may also have readily identified several persons in the congregation who can be of help to you. It's also possible, however, that you are wondering what on earth you can do for growth given some of the attitudes in your congregation. Even if no one wants to cooperate with you at the present time, there are some specific things you can start doing to work for growth:

- The most important single step you can take as an individual is to invite someone you know, who is not actively involved in a local church, to worship with your congregation.

- Learn to talk favorably about your local church around those who are not part of the congregation. Don't lie about the shortcomings of your church, but identify and share the strengths.

- If you want to make a difference in church growth, whether you are a church professional or a lay volunteer, start making visits to the homes of prospective members.

- Cultivate a personal attitude of genuine interest in and concern for prospective members combined with a sincere desire to share the love of Christ and of the church.

- Start sharing your concern about church growth with other members of your congregation. You may wish to give people copies of a book like this one. You may also wish to start researching the history of growth or decline in your congregation and sharing that information with others.

- Invite a Sunday school class or a small group to share with you in a study on the topic of church growth.

- Work toward the creation of an ad hoc long-range planning committee for your church, which can be a good means for identifying the overall needs of your congregation.

- Always remember that we are the agents through whom God may choose to speak to the hearts and minds of others, but God is the one who changes the hearts, minds, and lives of people. Our work in church growth needs to be supported by a life of regular prayer, Bible study, and meditation.

The preceding concepts are also discussed, in slightly different form, in my book *Plain Talk About Church Growth*.

A Thirteen Week or Ninety-two Day Experiment

While effective church growth is not a short-term process, it's sometimes useful to start a church growth initiative with a combination of study and action. If you are starting work on church growth concerns without a good support base in your congregation, then such study groups can be a very effective means to win the support of others. This outline can be used with a class, committee, or task force that is ready to look at church growth issues. The thirteen week time-frame is suggested since that is the length of a quarter for many Sunday school classes and small groups. There are actually suggestions for a total of fourteen group meetings, but the last one could be eliminated. Some groups will not be ready to do the amount of visiting in homes that is suggested. This book and the Bible are the basic resources.

Day One - Group Meeting One: Discuss "A Familiar Story" from this book and *Matthew 28:16-20* (which shares Christ's commission to reach out to others).

Days Two Through Seven: Suggest that each member of the group take the initiative to invite one friend, neighbor, or coworker to attend worship services the following Sunday.

Day Eight - Group Meeting Two: Discuss "Facing Reality: Demographics and Growth" from this book and *Mark 6:30-44* (which does show that numbers were not ignored in the gospel accounts).

Days Nine through Fourteen: Suggest that each group member visit with one or two older members of the congregation to gain their perspective on growth and decline in the church and on the history of the ministry area in which the church is located. Have one or two members research the official membership roles and census records to obtain some of the data suggested in the chapter studied on Day Eight.

Day Fifteen - Group Meeting Three: Spend the session sharing the information people obtained during the week and studying *Luke 10:1-12* (which emphasizes the importance Jesus attached to what those who followed him could accomplish and describes people being sent out in pairs).

Days Sixteen Through Twenty-one: Have group members work in pairs to interview persons who are on the membership roles of your church but who are no longer attending. The information gained from these interviews may help you in better understanding why some people break the habit of regular church attendance.

Day Twenty-two - Group Meeting Four: Have people share the results of their visits during the week and study *Luke 15:1-7* (on the Lost Sheep).

Days Twenty-three Through Twenty-eight: Have members continue to work in pairs on visits to inactive members.

Day Twenty-nine - Group Meeting Five: Discuss "Overcoming Low Self-Esteem" from this book and *I Corinthians 12:1-31* (on spiritual gifts).

Days Thirty Through Thirty-five: Have all group members work during the week to make lists of: their own strengths and weaknesses; the strengths and weaknesses of your local church; and the strengths and weaknesses of your denomination. The length of the lists should be up to each person - but there must be as many strengths listed as weaknesses for each category!

Day Thirty-six - Group Meeting Six: Have group members share the lists they developed during the week, keeping the emphasis on strengths rather than weaknesses, and study *Luke 10:25-37* (in which we are told to love our neighbors as we love ourselves).

Days Thirty-seven Through Forty-Two: Have group members individually, or in pairs, interview others in the congregation to find out what strengths and weaknesses those persons see in your church.

Day Forty-three - Group Meeting Seven: Have group members share the results of their interviews and study *1 Corinthians 12* (on the church as the body of Christ).

Days Forty-four Through Forty-nine: Have group members collect examples of positive attitudes and negative attitudes from books, newspaper articles, television shows, motivational tapes, etc.

Day Fifty - Group Meeting Eight: Have group members share the examples they've collected. Then discuss "Overcoming Negative Attitudes" and study *John 5:1-18* (on Jesus refusing to submit to negative attitudes about healing on the sabbath).

Days Fifty-one Through Fifty-six: Have group members work prayerfully during the week to identify lists of persons who (1) are prospective members for the church and (2) are members of the church who might be enlisted to help in church growth efforts.

Day Fifty-seven - Group Meeting Nine: Pull together the lists people have developed during the week. Then discuss "Overcoming a Shortage of Volunteers" and study *John 8:31-38* (on true disciples).

Days Fifty-eight Through Sixty-three: Have group members begin working in pairs to visit in the homes of persons on the list of prospective members.

Day Sixty-four - Group Meeting Ten: Have group members share their feelings about the calls they made. Discuss "Overcoming Limited Advertising Resources" and study *John 6:1-15* (another report on the feeding of 5,000).

Days Sixty-five Through Seventy: Have group members do research on the church's advertising strategies, including investigation of newspaper, radio, and television possibilities as appropriate.

Day Seventy-one - Group Meeting Eleven: Share results of the research done on advertising, and note any recommendations the group wishes to make to other organizations in the church. Discuss "Another Look at Entry Points" and study *I Corinthians 13* (on love as the center of all that we do).

Days Seventy-two Through Seventy-seven: Have group members do another round of visiting on prospective members, this time being especially sensitive to the entry points they might suggest to these persons.

Day Seventy-eight - Group Meeting Twelve: Share results of the visits. Discuss "Overcoming Inadequate Visitor Follow-Up" and study *John 10:1-21* (on Jesus as the Good Shepherd, as related to the importance of following up on those who attend).

Days Seventy-nine Through Eighty-four: Have group members make calls on persons who have visited your church over the last six months. Have them learn why those persons came, how those persons felt the church responded to them, and what decision those persons have made concerning church membership. These visits will probably be too late to reverse things with any who did not receive prompt follow-up; but they are not too late for group members to better understand how visitors perceive the church.

Day Eighty-five - Group Meeting Thirteen: Share results of the visits. Discuss "Overcoming Difficult Assimilation" and study *1 Corinthians 3:1-23* (about divisions in the Corinthian church which had not properly integrated all members).

Days Eighty-six Through Ninety-one: If you will not be having a fourteenth group meeting, then suggest that group members continue to work on visits to prospective members. If you will be having a fourteenth group meeting, then you may wish to shift their focus to interviewing persons who have become members of your congregation during the past ten years to see how they view the church and the extent to which they feel integrated into the congregation.

Day Ninety-two: Share results of the visits made by group members. Discuss "Building Quality" and study *Matthew 7:24-29* (on building a firm, "quality" foundation for our lives as individuals and in the church).

Resources

The books listed below are available from The Andrew Center. Send your order to The Andrew Center, 1451 Dundee Avenue, Elgin, Illinois 60120, or call 1-800-774-3360.

Riding the River - *Congregational Outreach and the Currents of the 21st Century* by Paul Mundey examines some of the most significant changes projected for our society and explores the implications of those transitions for the local church. R0455 $5.95

Fifty Ways to Reach Young Singles, Couples, and Families by Steve Clapp offers tested, practical ways for reaching out to young adults in a variety of life situations. R0457 $6.95

Reaching Out Through Christian Education by Steve Clapp and Jerry O. Cook draws on experiences in local churches across the country to give you the handles you need to revitalize your church's educational program and in the process the whole congregation. R0458 $12.95

Change and the Established Congregation by Paul Mundey grows out of The Andrew Center's extensive research on change. Issues studied include worship innovation, staffing changes, building and renovation programs, church growth programs, and outreach emphases. R0456 $11.95

Ministry with Young Adults - The Search for Intimacy edited by Julie Garber is a practical handbook for churches wanting to attract young adults (ages 18-35) and involve them in the faith community. Explores the needs of young adults and how to meet those needs through classes, groups, retreats, and leadership roles. R8733 $7.95

Promising Results by Steve Clapp tells the story of a process for change and growth at the congregational level called Passing On the Promise. A revised, nondenominational version of that process is being released in 1995. *Loren Mead of the Alban Institute* wrote about this book: "Its practical ideas and helpful information can help any congregation's leaders who want to move begin to grow." R8990 $4.95

How to Build a Magnetic Church by Herb Miller, one of the top church consultants in the country, shares time-tested, creative ways to draw new members and to nurture the whole church. R7626 $9.95

Strategies for Change by Lyle Schaller provides deep insight into the number-one issue facing Christian organizations today: *the need to initiate and implement planned change.* This book squarely faces barriers to change and shares valuable guidance. R0464 $11.95

More Than Numbers: The Way Churches Grow by Loren B. Mead explores what church growth and evangelism mean in a time when it may not be realistic for every congregation to achieve significant numerical growth. R0465 $10.95

The Inviting Church: A Study of New Member Assimilation by Roy M. Oswald and Speed B. Leas will help your church assess its assimilation process and understand how outsiders see the church. R0466 $11.95

Developing Your Small Church's Potential by Carl S. Dudley and Douglas Alan Walruth describes positive strategies for change and for absorbing new members. R5974 $9.00

Plain Talk About Church Growth by Steve Clapp offers practical advice for churches serious about growth. R8089 $12.95

How to Mobilize Church Volunteers by Marlene Wilson offers ways to increase the number of volunteers available and to improve their performance and satisfaction. R0525 $11.95

Dare to Grow by C. Wayne Zunkel is a hands-on guide which offers a biblical foundation for building a healthy church. R0443 $16.95

The titles which follow are not available from The Andrew Center, but we also strongly recommend these materials:

Quest for Quality in the Church by Ezra Earl Jones tells how to change systems within the church in order to improve overall quality. Focused especially on the United Methodist Church but applicable to any denomination. *Discipleship Resources.*

Weaving the New Creation by James W. Fowler talks about stages of faith in personal spirituality in relationship to the ministry of the church. *HarperCollins.*

Twelve Keys to an Effective Church by Kennon L. Callahan has become a classic book on improving ministry and reaching out through the church. *HarperSanFrancisco.*

Biblical Perspectives on Evangelism by Walter Brueggemann presents a truly enlightening look at how we understand evangelism in the church and in the world. *Abingdon.*